So Ancient and So New

So Ancient and So New

St. Augustine's *Confessions* and Its Influences

Edited by Glenn Arbery

ST. AUGUSTINE'S PRESS
South Bend, Indiana

Manufactured in the United States of America.

1 2 3 4 5 6   25 24 23 22 21 20 19

Library of Congress Cataloging in Publication Data
Names: Arbery, Glenn C. (Glenn Cannon), 1951- editor.
Title: So ancient and so new :
St. Augustine's Confessions and its influences
/ edited by Glenn Arbery.
Description: 1st [edition].
South Bend, Indiana : St. Augustines Press, 2016.
Identifiers: LCCN 2016012547
ISBN 9781587318191 (paperbound : alk. paper)
Subjects: LCSH: Augustine, Saint, Bishop of Hippo. Confessiones.
Augustine, Saint, Bishop of Hippo.--Influence.
Classification: LCC BR65.A62 S65 2016 | DDC 270.2092--dc23 LC
record available at http://lccn.loc.gov/2016012547

∞ The paper used in this publication meets the minimum
requirements of the American National Standard for Information Sciences -
Permanence of Paper for Printed Materials, ANSI Z39.48-1984.

St. Augustine's Press
www.staugustine.net

Table of Contents

Preface

The study of any masterpiece can change one's life, but the *Confessions* of St. Augustine, like Plato's *Republic* or Dante's *Commedia*, has the almost uncanny power to enact in the reader what it describes. Plato's book reconfigures the city of the soul by freeing it from enslavement to the tyrannical passions and making it answerable to reason in its pursuit of the good. For Augustine, who shares many of the same ends, the pursuit of the good is not the rectification of philosophical reason, but (as it was for Dante) an intensely personal and consuming love: the encounter with the living God. Oddly, it may seem, that encounter comes for Augustine through the act of reading. Unlike Plato, who depicts the process of reasoning toward the truth, Augustine finds the truth revealed in another, immeasurably greater *book* that cannot be read in its true sense without the help of its author.

To break open Augustine's book in the early 21st century is to smell the fresh bread on the table at Emmaus. This little book of essays arose from that sense of discovery and celebration. Assumption College owes its very origins to the conversion recounted in Augustine's pages. Emmanuel d'Alzon, the founder of the Augustinians of the Assumption, patterned his understanding on St. Augustine, and in the spring of 2011, following upon the celebration of the 200th anniversary of d'Alzon's birth, the college plumbed the sources of its intellectual and spiritual life with a two-day conference on the *Confessions* and its influence on later thinkers. It was primarily an occasion to deepen understanding and foster conversation within the college itself. But right away, after two or three papers, it was evident that this effort could not end as merely an in-house exercise. Rather, in something like the spirit discussed by Dan Maher in his essay on Augustine's motives for sharing his confessions, these meditations needed to be made public, not because they add indispensably to scholarship on the *Confessions*, but because they embody what happens in fresh encounters with this seminal book. They are themselves a species of confession, and as such, they are a provocation to rediscover the beauty "so ancient and so new" that inheres in a text apparently so distant from a world bent above its technologies and forever texting.

The essays uncover a variety of themes, from Augustine's act of reading (LePain and Bercier), his emphasis on memory (Corriveau), and his choice to reveal to the world his "hidden and unworldly activity" (Maher), to the way Augustine's own education might serve as a corrective to contemporary understandings of "assessment" (Colvert). The vast wake of Augustine's work includes writers from Dante and Montaigne to Nabokov, but faculty chose three representative figures to show his influence: Jean-Jacques Rousseau in the *Confessions* (Sorenson), James Joyce in the whole range of his work (Knowlton), and T.S. Eliot in the *Four Quartets* (Arbery). The most direct engagement with Augustine is obviously Rousseau's. In his essay comparing and contrasting the pivotal moments of the two *Confessions*, Rick Sorenson explores major differences between the way of faith and the path of reliance on reason. Joyce might be said to have taken Rousseau's path (at least in rejecting revelation), whereas Eliot took Augustine's.

In its sophistications and anxieties, the late antiquity Augustine inhabited feels a great deal like the late modernity we inhabit now. Certainly, the barbarians of materialist thought long ago sacked the civilization our ancestors inhabited. When Eliot published *The Waste Land* in 1922, he already saw the old order of antiquity and Christendom as "stony rubble," "a heap of broken images." As one of his speakers puts it, "Dry bones can harm no one." This old book, the *Confessions*, might seem to our contemporaries as dry and dead as those bones, but it is not so.

Without being a defense of Christianity (as the *City of God* is) or a work of catechesis, the *Confessions* might be the greatest counter to the materialist creed in Western literature. It recounts Augustine's central, intensely personal, and ultimately liberating struggle to conceive of spiritual substance, an intellectual achievement without which he cannot even hope to accommodate his understanding to the reality of God. This book of essays has one primary end, which is to entice the reader to reopen Augustine's book, to look over his shoulder and see what the act of reading means to him and what it has accomplished: the world-changing encounter with the substance of the Word.

Glenn Arbery
Lander, Wyoming

}x{

Reading Augustine Reading
Marc A. LePain

A book that speaks of reading books is not a rarity among the books we read. Haven't we read in Dante's *Comedy* Francesca recall how she and Paolo "read no more that day" they were reading of the love of Lancelot and Guinevere? Haven't we read in *Don Quixote* how reading books of chivalry made a madman of Cervantes' hero? Haven't we read Pao-yu read novels of Yang Kuei-fei instead of the Confucian books in *Dream of the Red Chamber*? It seems that Virginia Woolf got it right when she told of sometimes dreaming that "when the Day of Judgment dawns ... the Almighty will turn to Peter and will say, not without a certain envy when He sees us coming with our books under our arms, 'Look, these need no reward. We have nothing to give them here. They have loved reading'."[1]

If you haven't read that curious work Augustine called his "Confessions," perhaps you will now want to read it. There's a saying I heard often in my student days, "Tell me what you read and I will tell you who you are." A French writer of the last century, François Mauriac, observed that while that is true, "I will know you better if you tell me what you re-read."[2] Perhaps the many among you who have read Augustine's *Confessions* will want to re-read the work.

---

1   Virginia Woolf, *The Common Reader*, Second Series (New York, 1932), 245.
2   "'Dis-moi ce que tu lis, je te dirai qui tu es...' Il est vrai, mais je te connaîtrai mieux si tu me dis ce que tu *relis*." François Mauriac, *Mémoirs intérieurs* (Paris, 1959), 138.

How are we to read this book? The way Augustine expected us to read it? For him reading meant reading aloud, with not only our mind and our eyes, but our tongue and our ears also engaged in the act of reading. This means fewer distractions to intrude on our concentration: neither sound nor screen in the background or foreground. It also means we read slowly to sound the syllables that become words and sentences in sequence: no speed-reading here, and no mental indigestion either. Let us recall Augustine's puzzled reaction to bishop Ambrose's strange reading habit: "When he read his eyes would travel across the pages and his mind would explore the sense, but his voice and tongue were silent ... It was never otherwise." At a loss to understand why Ambrose read this way Augustine gives him the benefit of the doubt and concludes that "whatever his reason, that man undoubtedly had a good one" (VI,3,3).[3]

How are we to understand the title Augustine chose for his book? For most of us the term confession first conjures an acknowledgement of wrongdoing, of crime or sin depending on the context, and most memorably in the *Confessions* Augustine's account of his theft of pears. The term also calls to mind an acknowledgment of belief or profession of faith; there is certainly some of that too in the *Confessions*. But neither of these is what Augustine meant by the title he chose. Even if we consult a dictionary we are not likely to find Augustine's meaning there, a sign that in the course of time we have lost it.

He tells us in the *Revisions* he composed near the end of his life "the thirteen books of my *Confessions* praise the just and good God for both the bad and the good that I did, and they draw a person's mind and emotions toward him"[4] (II,6). Perhaps we missed that note of praise in the opening line's citation of Psalm 48: "Great are You, o Lord, and exceedingly worthy of praise," "*Magnus es,*

---

3   Passages from the *Confessions* of Augustine are cited from the English translations by either Maria Boulding, OSB, or John Ryan, according to Book, chapter, and numbered paragraph.

4   Augustine, *Revisions* II,6 (33), trans. Boniface Ramsey (New York, 2010), 114.

domine, et laudablis valde" (I,1,1). Augustine, it is often observed, invented a genre of writing that had no precedent and perhaps fewer imitators than we like to imagine since he did not properly speaking compose an autobiography. Rather, Augustine's *Confessions* constitute one long prayer of praise to God in the biblical sense of confession as praise.

In these *Confessions* we find numerous instances of Augustine describing how what he read changed his mind and his heart. These accounts all appear within the first nine books of the *Confessions*. They are already well known to many of you but they are worth recalling here, if only to impress upon us the power the written word exerted on Augustine and, by implication, the force his own writing might exert on us who read what he wrote.

Leaving aside his early schooling, where the primary text was the *Aeneid* of Virgil, the Roman poet that he would engage again at a later date, the first instance of a decisive reading experience is undoubtedly Augustine's encounter with the *Hortensius* of Cicero, an exhortation to philosophy that he read in the course of his studies in rhetoric. Through that book's call Augustine "was aroused and kindled and set on fire to love and seek and capture and hold fast and strongly cling not to this or that school, but to wisdom itself, whatever it might be" (III,4,8). Echoing the return of the prodigal son, Augustine says he "began to rise up, in order to return to [God]" (III,4,7). Twelve years later, he recalled the turning point that reading Cicero had been for him.

Cicero's call to love wisdom could only go so deep in the soul of the young Augustine, for it lacked mention of the name of Christ he had taken in with his mother's milk. Even then, he recalls, "No writing from which [the name of Christ] was missing ... could ever captivate me completely" (III,4,8). Accordingly, Augustine turned to the Bible to fill the lacuna in Cicero's book. The result was disappointing, above all because his "swollen pride recoiled from its style and my intelligence failed to penetrate to its inner meaning. Scripture is a reality that grows along with little children, but I disdained to be a little child and in my high-and-mighty arrogance regarded myself as grown up" (III,5,9).

Since Scripture was a dead end and Cicero did not satisfy fully, Augustine turned to the Manichees, whose dualistic doctrine included biblical elements and would engage his attention for some nine years. Augustine's Manichean turn so concerned his mother that she tried to prevail on a Catholic bishop, himself a former Manichee, to convince her son otherwise. The bishop's advice was to "leave him alone ... He will find out for himself through his reading" (III,12,21). In the course of time, this is exactly what happened. Augustine recalls how he had "read widely" in the works of philosophers: "I began to compare certain elements from my reading with the long-winded myths of the Manichees. The philosophers' conclusions seemed to me more probable, since these men had been clever enough to make calculations about the world" (V,3,3).

In the course of these years when he was about twenty years of age, Augustine also came upon "a certain writing of Aristotle ... entitled *The Ten Categories*." His intellectual thirst was such that "at the very name of the book I would hang on [my teacher's] words agape, as though expecting some important divine revelation." What is more, he "read them in private and understood them" without his teacher's help (IV,16,28). But looking back on his prideful disposition, Augustine now wonders "what profit that was to me ... No, the reading had been no profit to me – a hindrance, rather" (IV,16,28–29).

Of much more profit to Augustine was his reading of the books of the Platonists that were placed in his hands some years later in Milan. By that time he had begun to see Scripture in a better light, thanks to the preaching of bishop Ambrose, who taught Augustine the general Pauline principle that "the letter kills, but the spirit gives life" (II Corinthians 3.6) and corrected the erroneous view he held of humanity's being made in the image of God by showing him what the Catholic understanding truly was.

In a memorable comparison of the Bible with the books of the Platonists, Augustine says of the latter:

> In them I read (not the same words were used, but precisely the same doctrine was taught, buttressed by many

and various arguments) that in the beginning was the word, and the word was with God [...] But that he came to his own home, and his own people did not receive him; but to those who did receive him, he gave power to become children of God; to those, that is, who believe in his name – none of this did I read there. (VII,9,13).

Despite what was missing in those books Augustine saw in them the gold that the Israelites had brought out of Egypt and compared his find to what Paul had told the Athenians, "that in [God] we live and move and have our being and that indeed some of their own authorities had said this, and unquestionably those books I read came from there." (VII,9,15).

As he read Scripture further, he took up the Letters of Paul and contrasted the presumption induced by the books of the Platonists, which had been given him by "a man swollen with pride" and which he now referred to as "those books," with the humble confession brought about by "your books" (VII,20,26), as he calls the Bible, that taught not only the goal but the way to the goal. Yet this did not negate the truth he found in "those books." Indeed, in hindsight Augustine found it good that he had not first become well informed about Scripture. If he had, he says, "and then I had afterward chanced upon those other volumes, they might perhaps have torn me loose from the strong root of piety, or else, if I had held firm in the salutary devotion I had absorbed, I might have supposed that it could be acquired equally well from those books, if everyone studied them and nothing else" (VII,20,26). In reading Paul's letters after the Platonists' books he "discovered that every truth [he] had read in those other books was taught here also, but now inseparably from your gift of grace" (VII,21,27).

The love of wisdom to which Cicero's *Hortensius* had first converted him years before in Carthage now had come full circle in Augustine's assent of the intellect to the Truth of Christ. But there remained the consent of the will that he had not given to the Way to the Truth. Once again, that final turn came through reading a passage of St. Paul's Latter to the Romans that Augustine was brought to read when he heard a child's voice seem to cry, "*Tolle, lege*," "Take up and read." He was further prompted to take up and read when he recalled how in *The Life of Antony*, as Ponticianus told him his friend had read, Antony was converted upon hearing a Gospel passage read. Once Augustine had read the passage in Romans, he told his friend Alypius, who asked to see what Augustine had read and then pointed to the next verse, "Make room for the one who is weak in faith," which Alypius read to mean himself (VIII,12,29–30).

In light of the evidence adduced, at this point I might rest my case for reading Augustine reading. But there is more. Just as we read in the Inferno what Francesca says she and Paolo read but hardly ever get to read what Dante himself read in Paradiso, and just as we read about Troy and Dido in the first six books of Virgil's *Aeneid* but hardly ever read the latter six though Virgil asserts that "a greater theme is born for me; I try a greater labor" (VII,44–45), so we often overlook the last three books of Augustine's *Confessions* and some translations of the *Confessions* omit Books XI through XIII altogether. Yet these neglected books are by Augustine's own account of greater significance to his purpose.

In these books Augustine fulfills his office of bishop, which, along with administering the sacraments, consists of preaching the word to his flock, in this instance his readers. In fact, he says he had "long burned with desire to meditate" on the divine law (XI,2,2). By this time he had already composed the first of his five commentaries on Genesis, that one against the Manichees, and another on the Sermon on the Mount. The latter commentary was the fruit of his close study of Scripture during the free time he requested and was granted by his bishop just after his priestly ordination.

Like the woods that beckon and harbor deer, the prospect before him of Scripture's many "obscure and secret" pages is broad and deep but the reward will be great, for "not in vain do deer seek shelter in those woods, to hide and venture forth, roam and browse, lie down and ruminate" (XI,3,3). Augustine's purpose in these last books is to "confess all that I have found in your books, to hear the voice of praise and drink from you, from the beginning when you made heaven and earth to that everlasting reign when we shall be with you in your holy city" (XI,3,3).

Contrary to what some might expect, Augustine does not proceed to read the whole of Scripture, from the creation in Genesis to the heavenly city in Revelation. Rather, he meets his intended objective through a careful reading of the opening page of the Bible, of the Genesis creation story in seven days. His reading of this first account forms the common thread in these last three books though we might say the weaving is uneven. Books XI and XII together deal with Genesis 1.1–2 only, which comes in our editions to sixty pages of text devoted to explaining just two verses of the Bible. Only in the last book does Augustine take up the rest of the creation account.

These books also evince a Trinitarian pattern, with a focus on God the Father and the mystery of God's eternity and created time in Book XI, on the Son as the beginning or principle of creation in Book XII, and on the Spirit at work in creation in Book XIII. As Augustine reads through the Genesis creation story, so also he moves from one divine Person to another until his work culminates with the Spirit's action in bringing us to the seventh day of rest.

Augustine's aim in these books is to understand the Scripture: "Let me listen and understand how you made heaven and earth in the beginning." But "who can understand this? Who explain it?" he asks (XI,3,5). The challenge lies in the gulf that separates Creator and creature, a gap that fills Augustine "with horror and longing: with horror inasmuch as I am unlike him; with longing inasmuch as I am like him" (XI,9,11).

Time itself does not allow us to give full attention to the subject of Book XI. Indeed, as I speak this sentence and anticipate how it will end, no sooner have I spoken it than my sentence becomes a memory of past words spoken. This whole talk is in tension between its conclusion and beginning, at every point looking ahead at what is about to be said and looking back at what has just been said. "The same thing happens in the entirety of a person's life," Augustine observes, and, he adds, "the same [happens] in the entire sweep of human history" (XI,28,38). Our life is lived in distention between future and past in ever flowing present.

But the Word of God become human alters this human experience of time by giving Augustine a goal toward which to direct himself, "so that I may be gathered in from dispersion in my former days to pursue the One, forgetting the past and stretching undistracted not to future things doomed to pass away, but to my eternal goal. Without distention but with intention I press on to the prize of our heavenly calling" (XI,29,39).

Within time, as a pilgrim on the way toward this goal Augustine seeks to understand God's creation. As Book XII opens, he says he is occupied with "many things" concerning Scripture and acknowledges that the task of understanding requires painstaking effort on the part of the reader and even more for the one who speaks and writes of what he reads, for "to seek requires more talking than to find, to ask takes longer than to obtain, and the hand that knocks puts in more effort than the hand that receives" (XII,1,1)

Let us follow Augustine in his effort to understand the opening words of Genesis. At the time he writes, Augustine's understanding is that the heaven and earth God created are two kinds of creature, the one perfectly formed, the other lacking any form; neither of them affected by the passage of time although neither is coeternal with God. The one, heaven, the *caelum caeli* or "heaven's heaven," is "so formed that without any slackening in its contemplation, without any intervening period of change, and without suffering any mutation in itself in spite of its mutability, it finds its total fulfillment in your eternal immutability." The other, earth, was created "so formless that it lacked all capacity to be changed from one form to another." From this earth, "formless and void," were to be made another heaven, the vault of the sky, and the visible, organized earth in a succession of days needed to "bring about ordered modifications of motion or form" (XII,12,15).

Augustine is aware of other possible ways to read these same words. But, he says, "what does it matter to me if what I think the author thought is different from what someone else thinks he thought? All of us, his readers, are doing our utmost to search out and understand what the writer we read willed to say." Augustine goes further, asserting that it is possible to understand a meaning in these words that was not present in the mind of the human author, Moses, since the source of meaning lies beyond Moses in Truth itself. "What harm is there," he asks, "if a reader holds an opinion which you, the light of all truthful minds, show to be true, even though it is not what was intended by the author, who himself meant something true, but not exactly that?" (XII,18,27).

As an illustration of this principle Augustine cites several alternative meanings first of these opening words and then of the words that follow, noting for the first how

> one person picks out one meaning to explain the words *'In the beginning God made heaven and earth,'* and says, 'This means that in his Word, coeternal with himself, God made both intelligible and sensible creation, or spiritual and corporeal.' Another chooses differently: *'In the beginning God made heaven and earth'* means that in his Word, coeternal with himself, God made the whole vast bulk of this corporeal world, together with all the array of natures known to us which it contained." Another adopts a different interpretation again: *'In the beginning God made heaven and earth'* means that in his Word, coeternal with himself, he made the formless matter underlying his spiritual and material creation.' Another view is taken by the one who says, *'In the beginning God made heaven and earth'* means that in his Word, coeternal with himself, God made the formless matter of his corporeal creation; contained within it in a still confused state were the heaven and earth which in this vast world we now perceive as distinct and formed.' Yet another takes the view that *'In the beginning God made heaven and earth'* means that at the very inception of his making and working God made the formless matter which contained heaven and earth in a confused state, and from it they now stand forth plain to see, together with all that is in them" (XII,20,29).

In light of his review of "so rich a variety of very truthful meanings" Augustine summons his reader to "consider how foolish it is rashly to assert that Moses intended one particular meaning rather than any of the others." Augustine calls for a community of readers, gathered in what we could call a celebration of reading what Moses wrote and bound, Augustine insists, by charity, "for the sake of which he said all those things" (XII,25,35).

If he had been in the place of Moses, Augustine muses,

> and the task of writing the Book of Genesis had been upon me, I would have wished that such a gift of eloquence should be given me, and such skill in weaving words, that readers, unable to understand how God creates would not reject what I said as too difficult for them, while those who could already understand it, whatever might be the true idea they had arrived at by their own reasoning, should not find that their idea had been overlooked in your servant's few words. Finally I would hope to have written in such a way that if anyone else had in the light of truth seen some other meaning, that too should not be excluded, as a way of understanding the same words. (XII,26,36)

What Moses wrote is for Augustine "a spring whence rivers of limpid truth gush forth. Everyone draws for himself whatever truth he can from it about these questions, each a different point, and then hauls his discovery through the meandering channels of his own discourse, which are somewhat longer" (XII,27,37). In the terms of another metaphor, for mature readers the words of Scripture are no longer a nest whose humble mode of discourse cradles the weakness of promising children as though in their mother's arms, but "shady thickets in which they see hidden fruit. They fly to and fro joyfully, chattering as they search it out, and plucking it" (XII,28,38).

The scope of Augustine's concern broadens considerably in Book XIII as he comes to the third person of the Trinity and completes his reading of the creation account. We can picture him searching over the page of Genesis until he exclaims, "Ah, there was your Spirit poised above the waters!" (XIII,5,6). Beyond his first reading of the text, he now reads how "among us too has God in his Christ made heaven and earth" (XIII,12,13), for "we ourselves … were once turned away from you who are Light; in that earlier life we were darkness, and even now we labor … until in your only Son we become your righteousness" (XIII,2,3).

Augustine goes on to read the creation account allegorically as the story of the reformation of humanity, beginning with the first day when God summons to conversion the earth "formless and void" that is sinful humanity: "Let there be light; repent, for the kingdom of heaven is near, repent, and let there be light" (XIII,12,13). Here and again later Augustine cites St. Paul's admonition in Romans 12.2: "Do not be conformed to this world, but be transformed by the renewal of your mind" (XIII,13,14).

The vault God makes on the second day to separate the waters above and below is the book of Scripture. The sky will one day be rolled up like a book, but for the present it is stretched out above us for us to read of God's mercy manifested in created time. Beyond, in the waters above the vault, the angels behold the face of God and read His eternal will without the aid of time-bound human words.

The bitter seas of sinful humanity gathered on the third day allow the earth that is redeemed humanity to come forth. As the earth is to bring forth seed of its own kind, so the redeemed grow fertile through the works of mercy they do in love of their neighbors.

The greater and lesser lights made on the fourth day are the bearers of wisdom and knowledge, respectively, firmly set in the vault that is Scripture to teach the distinction between the goods of the mind and sensible things. The moon and the stars illumine the night for those preoccupied with sensible matters, while the sun shines in daylight for those devoted to the life of the mind.

On the fifth day the birds above who fly close to the vault of Scripture are the messengers of good news and the fish in the waters below are the corporeal signs, both of which increase and multiply as the Church spreads through the world by means of preaching and the sacraments.

The sixth day is the day God creates human beings. But first come the land animals which are the impulses of the human soul that, like wild beasts made tame and gentle and subjected to reason, in keeping with St. Paul's injunction in Romans 12.2 to "not be conformed to this world" (XIII,21,30–31). This leads to the soul being "transformed by the renewal of [the] mind," as Paul enjoins in what he says next, a mind remade in the image of the Trinity of divine persons, as indicated by the plural God employs in creating human beings, "Let us make man in our image and after our likeness" (Genesis 1.26).

Those who are reformed and renewed and gifted with the Spirit judge of spiritual things, "not only ... the holders of spiritual authority but also those who are subject to them in the Spirit," which is the meaning of humanity created male and female, since "in respect of bodily sexuality male and female here have no significance, any more than do differences between Jew and Greek, slave and free. Spirit-filled persons, whether they rule or obey, judge in the light of the Spirit" (XIII,23,33).

Augustine notes that it is given to man to exercise dominion over the fish, the birds, and the land animals, but not over the lights set in the heavenly vault or the bitter waters of the sea. In the allegory of man's reformation dominion is exercised through the sacraments and by preaching, that, Augustine says, "through interpretation, exposition, discourse, disputation, blessing, or prayer ... in words subject to the authority of your book, like birds flying under the sky" (XIII,23,34).

God's command to "increase and multiply" that Augustine reads next is "a mystery" that makes him ask of God, "Are you giving us some kind of hint here?" (XIII,24,35). At pains to understand the meaning of these words, he confesses he does not believe that God "spoke in these terms to no purpose" and so he says he "will not pass over in silence the meaning that comes to my mind when this passage is read" and he does not "see what is to stop me responding sensitively to figurative expressions in your books" (XIII,24,36).

The command to increase and multiply, Augustine recalls, is given to fish and birds as well as to humans. This signifies how, on the one hand, something can be signified materially in many ways yet understood by the mind in only one way, as, for example, in the many ways one can fulfill the commandment to love. This corresponds to the blessing given to the fish and birds.

On the other hand, something else can be signified in one way but understood in many ways. For example, Scripture offers us a single truth, couched in many words, "In the beginning God made heaven and earth," but "is it not understood in many ways, not by deceit of error, by various kinds of true interpretations? This corresponds to the increase and multiplication of human progeny" (XIII,24,36), for "the fecundity of reason leads us to understand the breeding of humans as truths processed by the intelligence." Thus the blessing to "increase and multiply" gives us the power "both to articulate in various forms something we have grasped in a single way in our minds, and to interpret in many different senses something we have read." Human generation populates the dry land that signifies our "longing, the land where reason holds sway" (XIII,24,37).

Genesis further teaches that human beings were given for food "every plant yielding seed … and every tree with seed in its fruit" (Genesis 1.29). Here, with the help of what St. Paul says of his gratitude for the gifts of the Philippians, Augustine distinguishes "between gift and fruit. The gift is the actual things given by the person who supplies … necessary goods: it may be cash, food, drink, clothing, shelter." But the fruit that is the true cause of Paul's joy is "the good upright will of the giver." Our spirit, too, "feeds on what gives it joy," which is not the gift given but rejoicing in the fruit of the giver. (XIII,27,41–42).

Augustine brings his reading of Genesis to a close with the seventh day that has no evening. That day is the peace and rest that, Augustine says, "the voice of your book tells us beforehand that when our works are finished … we too may rest in you, in the

Sabbath of eternal life" (XIII,35,51), "that everlasting reign" as he said at the start of his reading, "when we shall be with you in your holy city" (XI,3,3).

By way of conclusion, I propose three considerations. First, regarding the overall structure of the *Confessions*. Augustine wrote the *Confessions* in such a way that the entire work moves toward a climax that comes in Book XIII, where Augustine's own story, told in the first ten books, is presented as part of the larger story of God's Spirit at work redeeming the world through Christ and His Church. The reading Augustine gives of the Genesis creation account in Book XIII provides the text in which Augustine can read his own life story. The many references Augustine makes to the story of the prodigal son in the early books point to the reading he gives in the last book of the creation story as the return or reformation of humanity to the image of God. As Fulbert Cayré, the Assumptionist founder of the Center for Augustinian Studies in Paris, observed, Augustine was in the habit of constructing works whose long development led up to a concentrated doctrinal synthesis, as he does in such other works as *De Magistro, De musica,* and *De Trinitate*.[5] Father Cayré's observation should persuade us that we are always the poorer for not reading the *Confessions* in their entirety.

Second, I propose that reading and writing be seen as a unifying theme in Augustine's *Confessions*. The question of the unity of the *Confessions* has become a commonplace in Augustinian studies. Along with others I think that the verbal acts of reading, speaking, and writing provide a thread that links the seemingly disparate parts of the *Confessions*: nine books about Augustine's past, wherein what he read informed his quest for Truth; a tenth book about his present state; and the last three his reading aloud as it were of Scripture's opening creation account. As Augustine tells us in Book I, his early schooling gave him the "power" to "read any piece of writing I come across and to write anything I have a mind

---

5   Fulbert Cayré, "Le Livre XIII des *Confessions* de S. Augustin," *Revue des études augustiniennes* II:1–2 (1956), 144.

to myself." In hindsight he now finds these skills more "honorable and fruitful" than the tales told by Virgil that captivated him as a schoolboy (I,13,20–21).

Against Socrates' depreciation of the art of writing in favor of spoken speech in Plato's *Phaedrus*, Augustine validates the written word of Scripture as the vault of the sky above us that God provides for us humans to read until we are able to read what the angels, who have no need of this written word, read. Augustine anticipates there will be reading in heaven, even for those of us who on the Day of Judgment will come with books under our arms. The books we loved to read here are not all there is to read. Our reading will be better there, yet it will be reading still. So we learn from a father of Western book culture, as Augustine has been called.[6]

Finally, Augustine helps us to appreciate both the strength and the weakness of language at the service of teaching and learning. What Augustine read shaped him in decisive ways and he would not seek to understand Scripture if it had nothing to teach him and those for whom he writes. Yet Augustine knows there are limitations to the words he speaks and writes as well as to the words God speaks in Scripture. Augustine made this clear in the only work of his he mentions by its title in the *Confessions*, the *De Magistro*, the dialogue *Concerning the Teacher* between himself and his son Adeodatus that Augustine refers to in his account of their baptism in Book IX. In their exploration of teaching and learning, father and son establish first that teaching does not occur without verbal signs, then that nothing is actually taught through signs without prior knowledge of the truth of things, and finally that Christ himself, the Word of God, is the Teacher of Truth within the human soul. Is it any wonder that the *Confessions* end with the author exclaiming, "What human will give to another to understand these things? What angel to another angel? What angel to a human? From you let it be asked. In you let it be sought. At your door let us knock for it. Thus, thus is it received, thus it is found, thus is it opened to us" (XIII,38,53).

6   See Brian Stock, *Augustine the Reader* (Cambridge, MA, 1996), 3.

The Mind of Augustine and the Rhetoric of God
By Barry Bercier, A.A.

The greatest literary influence on the *Confessions* of St. Augustine is the Bible. That's perfectly clear. The *Confessions* is not only a sort of montage of Biblical quotes, from beginning to end, but it is the story of Augustine's discovery of the Scriptures as the "firmament," as he calls it, the definitive authority stretched over him as the sky become an unfurled scroll, under which he comes to make his exodus from darkness and restless dispersion to peace, understanding and the happy life. He writes the *Confessions*, furthermore, to influence others also to come under that authority and so to make it their chief guide for the building of the City of God amidst the ruins of the dying empire of Rome.

The *Confessions* is, then, all about the reception of the Word of God and of the Scriptures. But as Augustine makes clear from the opening chapter of his book, reception of the Word is contingent on the Word's having been addressed to the one who is to receive it. "My faith prays to you, Lord, this faith which you gave me...through the Incarnation of your Son and through the ministry of the Preacher."[1]

Augustine was all his life preeminently a man of words. His birth is for him less a biological event than a verbal one, a sort of bursting into speech, "breaking in" his mouth, as he puts it, to the pronunciation of his first words, and from there "launching out into the stormy intercourse of human life."[2] But *logos* for Augustine was never to be merely a sort of tool...as it can be for the

1   *The Confessions*, Book I, chapter 1.
2   I, 1.

philosopher, that artisan of thought who imitates the structure of
being through the logical construction of words. Augustine was by
profession a rhetorician. For him words in their most proper function are the medium of communication among human beings, not
merely of some objective information one might have found, or of
some theoretical construct one might have built, but first and foremost words are for the communication of a *subjective* reality, the
inner life of those who would speak, the life of one's very identity
expressed in its desires, questions, convictions, its urge to understand and its drive to persuade, all concerning what is good, just,
and true. Such an inner life is not an objective natural phenomenon
to be observed but is of its very nature hidden unless the word be
expressed, spoken freely outward to whom one chooses freely to
reveal it. It is this free self-revelatory word that makes possible the
distinctively human life we live together. The "happy life" Augustine sought is such an inner, revealed and mutual life—of family,
friendship, community, and city.

The word or *logos* of such life is no sort of monadic emanation,
if I can put it that way. Rather it is, as part of its essence, a thing
received from others in one's relationship with them.

> I learned it in the caressing language of my nurses and in
> the laughter and play and kindnesses of those about me.
> In this learning I was under no pressure of punishment,
> and people did have to not urge me on; my own heart
> urged me on to give birth to the thoughts which it had
> conceived, and I could not do this unless I had learned
> some words; these I learned not from instructors but
> from people who talked to me and in whose hearing I
> too was able to give birth to what I was feeling.[3]

Now Augustine received the Word of Scripture in a most important
way through St. Paul. Paul is "the Preacher" he refers to in the
opening chapter of the book. Saul, the Jew, on his conversion

3   I, 14.

become Paul the Apostle, has as his work to carry the Word of God out from Israel and into the nations, the *goyim*, the pagans; Augustine, a citizen of that still largely pagan world, undergoes his conversion when he receives the Word from Paul and becomes a Christian. This I take to be the fundamental fact.

We should notice, then, that from the beginning, Augustine does not receive the Scriptures in precisely the same manner as do Moses and the People of Israel. The Jews across the ages see themselves as present with those gathered at Mount Sinai. With them Saul, too, received the Word from God who speaks to them directly, from the mountain within their midst. Saul received the Word as the Law which unites the people gathered together there on the holy ground of Sinai and thus creates Israel a nation even as it separates Israel out from all the other nations of the earth, just as God created light and separated it from the darkness. They become a people at once "set apart" from all others and the people set into a unique presence with God.

But then—and this is the mystery—it is precisely as a people set apart *from* all the nations that Israel is to be "holy," "peculiarly God's own" and "priestly," mediating the light of God's blessing *to* all the nations. This is what God promised Abraham, in a line Augustine quotes in *The City of God* when he asks the question "Who is the God...whom the Romans should have obeyed?" He answers the question: "He is the same God...from whom Abraham received the promise, 'Through you all the nations of the earth shall be blessed.'"[4] Augustine, then, stands as one among the nations, receiving the word of blessing from those who have been set apart from those very nations to give that blessing.

As another thinker influenced by Augustine would put it some eight centuries later, "whatever is received is received according to the mode of the receiver."[5] Augustine was to receive the word of Scripture not as the Law establishing the nation of Israel, but as the word addressed to the rest of us, us sorry pagans in deep need

4   XIX, 22; Genesis 12:3.
5   St. Thomas Aquinas, *Summa Theologica*, I, Q. xii, art. 4.

of a word to save us, even as we continue to live, for the most part, under the laws we make for ourselves and remain among the nations apart from Israel.

Augustine was to receive that word as one of us, or more to the point, as one who would sum up in himself, in his own vast heart, mind and memory, what it means for the pagan world to receive the word addressed to it from out of the soul of Israel. When Augustine "confesses" his reception of the saving word of God, that confession is paradigmatic for us all.

What Augustine learns to be his need, and the need of the dying Empire, the need that opens itself up to the Word, is what I'll try to get at in the next section of this paper. And for the final section, I'll try in the broadest possible stokes to sketch out how the "instruction that came forth from Zion and the Word of the Lord that came from Jerusalem"[6] was exactly the saving word to meet the pagan need.

* * *

Augustine had two great desires—he desired personal relationships and he desired wisdom. Over the course of his life, he gained clarity concerning those desires, and his other needs took shape relative to them. Or it might be better to say that Augustine came to live by one single desire, which we might call the desire for wise relationship, or for wisdom and truth in relationship...something like this.

From early on we see him aroused by Cicero's *Hortensius* to a burning desire for wisdom, a desire setting him on a lifelong course of intense inquiry and reflection. At every step along the course of his life others are there with him, necessary for him as he pursues wisdom and the happy life. His *Confessions* is a sort of autobiography composed of many biographies: that of his mother, his numerous friends, his students and his teachers, and others whose lives were models for him to consider, to emulate, or to reject.

Given his fiercely intense experience of relationships and

6   Isaiah 2:3.

communion as the very substance of life, mastery of the right practice of relationship would be a matter for him of great importance and of great difficulty as well. Augustine's sexual passions, therefore, were not an anomaly in his personality but were a necessary and vital component of it. It would take considerable doing to get them into proper order, but what was required for him, for his very salvation, was getting them into proper order, not ignoring or destroying them. They represented a real need in him, were an expression of his deepest desire, even if undirected they prevented its satisfaction.

Something similar can be said of the hungry energy of his intelligence. The restless journey of his mind, his insistence on coming to the truth of things, was not to be put to a halt by the docile acceptance of dogmatic conclusions reached by others. His mother would perhaps have had an easier time of it if Augustine had simply followed her wishes and been a good, believing boy from the beginning. But had he done so, his reception of the Word that was to be spoken to him from the deepest reservoirs and sources of Scripture into the deepest recesses of his heart and mind could not have taken place. We certainly wouldn't be talking about him sixteen centuries later, and those sixteen centuries themselves would have had a very different story to tell, because, given the vast scope of his intelligence, his perception of the relationships that might constitute a happy life was also made vast. Though he focused intensely on his particular circle of friends, he had a powerful gaze directed out toward the whole sweep of history—he had the mind of the Empire in which he lived.

The Empire mattered to him, first as the place for the realization of his ambitions, later as the cause of a deep dissatisfaction pressing him to separate himself from it, and finally as locus for the divine drama in which he and Rome would contend.

Augustine's desire for wisdom and relationship, then, would require of him the proper ordering of his sexual appetites, of his relationships with others, his public persona in the Empire, and most certainly the life of his mind. We see Augustine as a young man, however, struggling, sometimes desperately, with defects in each of these dimensions of his life. He gets too dependent on some of his friends. He doesn't know what to do with his mother. As he approaches success in his career as a rhetorician he suffers from powerful doubts about the worth of such a career and feels increasing disgust for the Empire into whose service he is about to sell himself. He would like to get away from it all, leading a leisurely intellectual life off with his friends, but his need for a sexual relationship binds him to family responsibilities which in turn bind him to a career and to the corruption of the Empire he would escape if he could. He feels stuck.

The intellectual effort he manages to make in the midst of these duties and distractions was, no doubt, of a prodigious sort relative to what most of us might think to take on. But still, for him, whatever his intellectual activity at the time, it was not satisfying. Augustine wanted a happy life with others in truth. He had to live his life with others well and rightly in truth. His desire for wisdom demanded nothing less, but this truth he could not seem to find.

One might say that as the political decline of Rome exposed the defects and flaws inherent in the Roman foundation from the beginning, making his public ambitions ultimately repugnant to him, so developments in the religious and philosophic institutions of Rome seemed to offer Augustine no hope of reaching the life-saving truth he sought. Rather, Augustine lived in a time like our own when it is only the experience of a generalized corruption that provides for many their first taste of wisdom.

Augustine, of course, knew early on the beauty of truth, but he knew as well some very ugly truths, and these made all the more difficult his journey to the truth that brings the happy life. It was not, however, only the corruption of Roman politics and culture that got him down, and not even his own disordered sexual passion as such that bothered him most. It was the terrible awareness that in himself, at the very core of his being, there was something seriously wrong. His discussion of his boyhood theft of the neighbor's pears is often enough taken as a sign that Augustine was too sensitive to feelings of guilt, but this misses the point. Augustine uses this objectively very minor event to reveal the otherwise hidden but enormous subjective event unfolding within him, making manifest a capacity in him for something entirely inexplicable in terms of a merely natural or philosophic understanding.

For the classical thinkers, people do bad things because their rational nature is deficient in education. Bad action is really only error. Knowledge is sufficient to make men good, whole and self-sufficient, or failing that, a Stoic detachment of will would suffice to deal with the bad things that come our way.

But Augustine knows from early on that something there is about him that does the bad thing knowingly, and that it is his will itself which, rather than detaching him from what is bad, chooses the bad and shows itself as therefore not merely bad, but evil. Augustine experiences evil as an interior and personal orientation of his willing self, for which philosophy can give no satisfying account or response. It is for this reason that he is attracted for a time to the Manicheans; they attempt to address the experience of evil. But as Augustine learns, the explanations they give are entirely unfounded, so that Augustine drifts for a long time in a most disquieting moral and intellectual twilight, stuck there, too.

His later encounter with the Platonists helps Augustine with a serious intellectual problem that had him stymied for a long time. The Platonists enable him to grasp the idea of immutability and immateriality so that he can better think both about his desire for abiding happiness and about the life of the soul that so desires. But the Platonists cannot deal with the problem of evil, nor do they point toward a happiness that can actually be achieved in the life human beings share with each other. The philosopher isn't defined by sharing his life but by self-sufficiency; he retires into abstraction and solitude or a small circle of friends. As Augustine puts it, while the philosopher points toward the happy life, he cannot attain it. Augustine makes this grotesquely clear in Book 19 of *The City of God* where he displays for the reader the plight of the aging philosopher who, having spent the time of his life in pursuit of wisdom as the knowledge of the whole and unchanging order of nature, is by that same natural order reduced to broken and crippled senility. While the philosopher seeks the immutable truth, time mutilates his flesh and unhinges his mind.

Philosophy cannot bring him the wisdom he desires. Augustine is still stuck.

What's left for him? Something his mother had managed to impress on him from his youth, and to which he responded in an enduring way, was her teaching him what he calls, "the name of Christ." Her attention to the person of Christ, to a *person* as the highest reality of all, resonated with Augustine, even despite his long refusal to take seriously the Scriptural tradition which taught that name.[7] That the highest wisdom should, so to speak, bear a human face was a thought that harmonized with Augustine's own desire for truth in relationship, a desire which decisively limited his interest in the Platonists.[8]

But serious inquiry into the Scriptural tradition was for a very long time not possible to Augustine. His classically formed intellectual powers, rhetorical skills, and literary tastes made the definitely unclassical forms of the Hebrew texts seem inferior to him. Classic thought, classic politics, and classic literature all took the flourishing of nature as their standard. Philosophic greatness, the achievement of poetic perfection, shining moral excellence, political glory—these are high standards, and according to them the Biblical texts simply do not measure up. To a man of the stature of the classical Augustine, the Scriptures might seem as primitive, barbaric, and unserious as, say, a Jewish tradesman or tent maker, hawking his wares in the Jewish Quarter of Rome...

But then again, Augustine had seen through the supposed grandeur of the classical world, that it was a fraud.

And then Augustine met Ambrose, Bishop of Milan. Ambrose, like Augustine, was a man of the word. He too was a fine rhetorician. Augustine, with the interest of a somewhat jaded professional, took to listening to the rhetoric of Ambrose as he preached, and at times spoke with him privately. Ambrose helped Augustine to see that the classical literary standards to which he was accustomed did not apply to the Scriptures, and this not because the Scriptures

7   VI, 4.
8   V, 14.

were defective but because they represented a different sort of discourse altogether. The Scriptures' standard of truth is not their imitation of the timeless perfection of nature. The Scriptures' authors do not aim at the glory due those who display their own perfection by the perfection of their works. Rather, the Scriptures address themselves to those who are humble, stuck in their own corruption and that of the world. The voice sounding through all the named and unnamed writers of Scripture speaks as one coming down, humbling himself, to be with the lowly and the fallen.

Hearing Ambrose, Augustine begins to open up to the possibility of the Scriptural Word that is from the Beginning, that is with God, that is God himself, who becomes flesh and dwells among us. Augustine looks to the People formed under the Scriptures and sees something altogether unlike Rome, a People who come to be precisely because in their patriarch Abraham, they left the empire of Babylon, and under their teacher Moses they left the empire of Egypt. He sees a nation that stands outside the sorry pattern of all the nations as he had experienced that pattern in Rome. He began to see before his mind's eye the People of God who are unlike Babylon, Egypt, and Rome not because they are inferior but because they stand in relation to the God who speaks with them and in whose company they too receive their word and learn to speak. What he discovers in that great unfurling of historical narrative found in the Scriptures is an account of the truth that does not flee life in time, as do the Manicheans, or that ignores it somehow in metaphysical abstraction, but that speaks *through* time, just as he himself might recite a poem or sing a song over time. Here is the truth that transcends time, but is revealed in time.

Most of all, the truth that is revealed in this way addresses itself to his own People. The truth of the happy life is not at an impossible remove, but comes and addresses itself to his People in time, now, past, present and future, as is the case in any personal self-revelation. The truth which Augustine had before sought through his own intellectual power, as Moses had sought to understand for himself the cause at work in the burning bush, Augustine began to realize is the truth that first knew him, just as it first knew Moses and called him by name and then revealed his own name to Moses: "And from far away you cried out to me: 'I am that I am.' And I heard as one hears things in the heart, and there was no longer any reason at all for me to doubt. I would sooner doubt my own existence than the existence of the truth 'which is clearly seen, being understood by those things which are made.'"[9]

Hearing this word sounding across the centuries enables Augustine to intuit for the first time something of the ultimate depth and substance that first stirred in him at his mother's mention of the name of Christ. Augustine decides to become a Christian at last. He wishes to receive the Word that is Christ addressed to himself.

This wish provokes the crisis. Though he is happy enough to leave behind his career and his old relationship to the Empire, what still binds his will is its attachment to the brokenness of his flesh. His longing for communion had for so long consoled itself with its sexual expression, a thing within his own power, that he could not let that consolation go. He had begun to see and to be convinced that his true consolation, the consolation of the Truth, was with the Word from the Beginning. But it was not enough to know that God had spoken, or even that he had spoken to all the nations through Israel in Christ. God had to address himself to him, in his own heart, and Augustine had to open himself to receive that address. He had to see and feel the sheer impossibility of saving himself—he had to give up that evil will, the will that was evil precisely because it was turned away from such a personal address; he had to know and to feel that his salvation, the communion and wisdom he desired, rested utterly in the will of another, of God and in God's free choice to address himself to Augustine. He had to abandon forever the claim of the sons of Adam to self-sufficiency.

It was in the garden under the fig tree that Augustine threw himself to the arms of God's grace.

He hears a child's voice, singing a little song, repeating the words *"tolle et lege,"* "take and read." He picks up a nearby text

9   VII, 10.

of St. Paul: "Not in rioting and drunkenness, not in sexual immorality and wantonness, not in strife and envy, but put on the Lord Jesus Christ and make no provision for the desires of the flesh."[10] He took it and read, and for the first time, he heard it as it was addressed and spoken to him: the Word from the Beginning, the Law at Sinai, the Word come to dwell among his People Israel, the Word made flesh in Christ, the Word addressed to the Jew Saul, the Letter of the Apostle Paul to the Romans, in the voice of child addressing the heart of a broken man, a Roman, weeping under the tree.

At once, the great desire of Augustine and its former needs are satisfied.

> And this is what you did: I was able totally to set my face against what I willed and to will what you willed...How glad I was to give up the things I had been so afraid to lose. For you cast them out and you entered into me to take their place, sweeter than all pleasure, but not to flesh and blood; brighter than all light, but more inward than all hidden depths; higher than all honor, but not to those who are high in themselves. Now my mind was free of those gnawing cares that came from ambition and the desire for gain and wallowing in filth and scratching the itchy scab of lust. **And now I was talking to you easily and simply, my brightness and my riches and my health, my Lord God.**[11]

Augustine's desire for truth and relationship is perfectly met by the living Truth, even the Word from the Beginning, Creator of all things, who has entered into relationship with him as person, not as object, but as the *other* who reveals himself to Augustine and to whom Augustine himself can speak. The personhood of God, God's relationship in otherness, known only in God's free self-revelation to us, is the truth and wisdom Augustine sought.

10 VII, 12. Romans 13:13–14.
11 IX, 9.

"Let me know you," he says, "even as I am known."[12] The desire for philosophic self-sufficiency in the claim to, or goal of, timeless knowledge, as an objective intellectual *seeing* of the supposed whole of things, is entirely reconfigured before the Truth that reveals itself to him, concretely, as a kind of speech that is heard, addressing itself to him. God's speech sounding in time and in the world and expressed most especially in the Scriptures, stretches like the skins of a scroll across the firmament of heaven,[13] replacing the supposed cosmic whole. For Augustine the cosmos is clearly not eternal and cannot be known as a whole, but rather it is fully immersed in time, entirely a process of one thing after another, just as is the sounding of speech itself. It is rendered fully intelligible only by the eternal truth and fidelity of the One who speaks, creates, and reveals himself to us through it. Playing off the image of Scriptural "skins," Scripture is the "lattice of flesh" he speaks of, alluding to the Song of Songs, when he says, "He looks through the lattice of our flesh, and he caressed us and set us on fire, and we run after his fragrance."[14] Scripture and the story of Israel teach the rhetoric of God as it breaks into speech in creation and across history and enters our hearts.

Likewise Augustine's understanding of the position of Rome in the world is transformed. Rome had claimed a political self-sufficiency which Augustine had come to see was fraudulent, but now he could see Rome as one of the nations, the many nations of the earth, not as universal world empire but as a neighborhood, so to speak, of the City of Man, known and judged by another, the New Jerusalem and the City of God. God's otherness, his unique personhood in relation to us, is revealed to us in the unique otherness of Israel, alone, set apart from all the nations, but created to be the one source of blessing to all the nations, as is manifested in Christ. A Christianized Rome then possesses knowledge of the one true God, *not* as a principle for claims to its own universal sovereignty,

12 X, 1.
13 XIII, 15.
14 XIII, 15; *Song of Songs*, 2:9.

and *not* as a sort of intrinsic principle of political motion and rest, but as an *extrinsic* principle, received from another, delegitimizing all claims to absolute or universal sovereignty.

Augustine's vast historical knowledge is thus reconfigured according to the pattern revealed in the Scriptures, and his own relationship to Rome is changed as well. Rather than selling his speech in praise of the emperor, he becomes bishop in the Church, establishing himself as *other* than the political order simply, and labors the rest of his life to open the people of his civilization to the knowledge of the living truth that transcends all politics and that, one way or another, transforms all politics as well. The concrete otherness of the People of Israel among the nations in history becomes the sacramental sign of the subordination of all political orders to the rule and judgment of the one, eternal, and transcendent God. Augustine's praise then rises to God, not the emperor.

The People set apart from all others, in Christ becomes the center of a new and lasting order of all things. The tranquil ordering of all things to the one God who reveals himself to us in history, this is the "peace" Augustine praises in the *The City of God*, true peace, the peace which he identifies with eternal life, replacing the supposed *Pax Romana* , and posing the definitive challenge to the succeeding political order we call Christendom.

In all these things Augustine becomes a sort of guide to his friends, and he becomes a perfect friend at last to his mother, as we see them shortly before her death, leaning by a window looking out onto a garden like the garden where he first received the word from St. Paul, speaking together in a moment of near-perfect communion with each other and with God.

The Once and Future Self:
Memory in Saint Augustine's *Confessions*
Roger R. Corriveau, A.A.

The "thin places" were those quiet, remote, solitary spots recognized by the Celtic mystics as being where God's wondrous presence is intensely experienced, those places where the veil between the Holy of Holies and this world is thin gauze shimmering with glints of God, those spellbinding thresholds between the seen and the invisible, the heard and the inaudible, the spoken and the ineffable, the common and the individual. Pilgrimage to the "thin places" of Ireland, England, Wales and Scotland has played an essential role in Celtic spirituality. When the Celts were barely beginning to turn to Christianity, Saint Augustine's *Confessions* were already revealing how intensely occupied he had been with the necessity of engaging oneself on pilgrimage. But his was the inward journey into himself. He found the gateway onto that inner road in his memory, the thinnest place possible, the crucible[1] where temporal and spatial realities as well as direct and indirect ways of knowing converged into his experience of God finding him there.

The Still-Point

To understand Saint Augustine's concept of memory,[2] we will often need to use our imagination, which is already an aspect of

1   Garry Wills, *Saint Augustine's Memory* (New York: 2002), 11.
2   We shall have to leave a far more extensive account of memory in the thought of Saint Augustine to others: See for instance: N. Cipriani, "Memory," in A. Fitzgerald, ed., *Augustine through the Ages: as En-*

memory as he understood it. Accordingly, we begin by visualizing a potter's wheel and imagining its utterly imperceptible "still-point," conceivable only as a theorem of geometry. Mathematics, incidentally, is also a matter of memory for Augustine.[3] The still-point of a potter's wheel is the very center of the wheel, which does not turn but from which the rest of the wheel spins. If a potter is going to throw a pot successfully, she must have mastered the art of centering the lump of clay on the still-point of the wheel. Failing to do so, as she begins to treadle her wheel, the sides of the pot emerging from her fingertips will wobble out of control and collapse.

The potter's wheel is a turning circle with a center, a circumference, and a radius stretching between both. The latter is a line that marshals an infinite number of points along itself, the first situated at the circle's center and the last at its circumference. As the radius rotates within the potter's wheel, the points closest to the wheel's circumference will travel a longer course at a greater speed to complete one revolution of the wheel than do the points closest to its center. The center of the spinning potter's wheel is the very first point of the radius, the still-point that neither moves within the circle nor turns on itself. The rest of the radius rotates from the still-point, so

cyclopedia, Grand Rapids: 1999), 553–555; J. Guitton, *Le temps et l'éternité chez Plotin et saint Augustin* ; E. Howells, "Appropriating the Divine Presence: Reading Augustine's *On the Trinity* as a Transformative Text," *Spiritus* 11 (2011): 201–223; G. Madec, "Memoria: Introspection et intériorié," in *Saint Augustin et le philosophie*, (Pairs: 1996), 85–91; A. Mourant, *St. Augustine on Memory* (Villanova: 1979); O'Daly, *Augustine's Philosophy of Mind* (Los Angeles: 1987), 131–151; A. Solignac, "La mémoire selon saint Asugustin (X, viii, 12 – xxvi, 37), *Bibliothèque Augustinienne* 14, 557–567; Id., "Memoria dans la tradition augustinienne," *Dictionnaire de Spiritualité* 10, 995–999; G. Wills, *Saint Augustine's Memory* (New York: 2002), 3–28; K. Winkler, "La théorie augustinienne de la mémoire à son point de départ," *Augustinus Magister* (Paris: 1954) 1, 511–519.

3   G. Ladner, *The Idea of Reform* (New York:1967), 212–222; O'Daly, 88; 179–183.

infinitesimally small that it has no dimension, and neither do the infinite number of points along the line of the radius.

Nothing happens at the still-point; everything else, fixed by the still-point, happens around it. In an analogy similar to the potter's wheel, in "Burnt Norton," the first of his "Four Quartets," T.S. Eliot provides a fitting account of the still-point:

At the still point of the turning world. Neither flesh nor fleshless;
Neither from nor towards; at the still point, there the dance is,
But neither arrest nor movement. And do not call it fixity,
Where past and future are gathered. Neither movement from nor towards,
Neither ascent nor decline. Except for the point, the still point,
There would be no dance, and there is only the dance. (ii, 62–67)

Augustine's memory flourishes in part from spatiotemporal experience, which is grounded in sensible perception, which in turn is activated in the measureless present moment. To understand the kind of remembering Augustine engaged in his *Confessions*, we will need to examine his concepts of time and then of memory. Both are still-points where nothing happens, but memory will turn out to be the thinnest of thin places, that still-point, that crucible where both time and space coalesce as human spirit.

To what extent did Saint Augustine know what time is?[4] He knew so long as no one asked him; when someone did, he could

4   We could refer to the following: L. Boros, "Les catégories de la temporalité chez saint Augustin," *Archives de Philosophie* 35 (1958): 323–85; K. Flasch, *Was ist Zeit? Augustinus von Hippo. Das XI Buch der Confessiones* (Frankfurt am Main, 1993); J. Guitton, *Le temps et l'éternité chez Plotin et saint Augustin* (Paris, 1959); G. Ladner, *The Idea of Reform* (New York: 1967), 203–212; 443–449; G. Madec, "Tempus – Aeternitas," in *Saint Augustin et la philosophie* (Paris: 1996), 93–99; G. O'Daly, *Augustine's Philosophy of Mind* (Los Angeles, 1987), 152–161; J. Quinn, "Four Faces of Time in St. Augustine," *Recherches Augustiniennes* 26 (1992): 181–231; A. Solignac, "La conception du temps chez Augustin," *Bibliothèque Augustinienne* 14 (Paris: 1963), 581–591; R. Teske, "The World-Soul and Time in St. Augustine," *Augustinian Studies* 14 (1983): 75–92.

not explain it (*Conf.* 11:14,17).[5] What we call the past has already gone by; it no longer exists and as such has no duration. What we call the future is not yet: it still does not exist and therefore has no duration. And what is the present? It is that evanescent point when the future, which does not yet exist, slips into the past, which no longer exists (11:15,19–20). The present only seems to have duration in time, but that duration is the measureless slipping of the future into the past (11:16,21)! The present is like that dimension-less still-point on the potter's wheel or at the center of a turning circle. As Augustine was dictating his *Confessions*, the first part of any sentence had already slipped into the past and the rest of it which was yet not spoken did not yet exist; and as soon as he stopped dictating his sentence at its period, the whole thing had slipped into the past. It had never existed in the present really, and it existed then only in the past, which was no longer.

So the time of the present has no duration (11:15,20) and lasts for as long as the center of a circle has width. The future slips through the flash point of the present and becomes the past. The present, as we usually think about it, has already slipped into the past as soon as we become aware of it. Augustine concludes that there are not three times: past, present and future. There are rather three presents: the present of the past, the present of the present, and the present of the future. All three exist in the presence of the memory (11:20,26). And the memory is measurelessly, fathomlessly extensive. It is as deep as the universe is old and as broad as the universe is expanding. The past, held in the vast caverns of memory, is always present; it is not even past (11:20,26). Since the present has no duration, nothing happens in the present, the still-point of time. Everything happens in memory's re-presentations.

Saint Augustine's idea of memory is that it is at once an active faculty and an almost infinitely "huge warehouse, the storage place of old experiences, a passive place of deposit, a kind of glorified dump,"[6] a spacious treasure trove of representations, experiences

5   Henceforth all unspecified citations will refer to the *Confessions*.
6   Wills, 3.

and imaginations stored for preservation (10:8,12). We can be quite disconcerted by Augustine's many meanings of memory that stray far from our modern psychological concepts of the human memory as the remembering of the past. Augustine's use of the word *memoria* applies to everything contained within the human spirit, even what is not necessarily consciously known or perceived. Even what we have forgotten remains nevertheless present through our awareness of having forgotten it (10:17,24), and we may even be able to retrieve it through our memory's attempt to remember it (10:19,28). The meaning of certain words we use so readily today, like the unconscious and the subconscious, need to be widened to include the metaphysical presence within the soul of transcendent realties, distinct from itself, like God.[7]

We shall limit ourselves to three categories of "things" contained in our memory's collection. One consists of those things that entered there when they were in the future, slipping through the still-point of the present into the presence of the past. Another is comprised of those things that came to be when we made them up with our creative imagination to be present. And a third category clusters those things which transcend all experience of a world outside of ourselves and all the imaginative constructions of a memory's world and actually establishes the possibility of the memory's experience and creative imagination.

Sense Experience

Saint Augustine may have come under the fortunate influence of the Milanese Platonists in his earlier life, but he was not entirely passive in his reception of Plato's characteristic distinction between the *sensibilia* and the *intelligibilia* (*Acad.* 3:19,42).[8] He understood that Platonism tended to establish two distinct worlds, that of matter and that of spirit. He knew all too well that the Manicheans

---

7   É. Gilson, *Introduction à l'étude de saint Augustin*, 3e éd. (Paris: 1949), 135, n.2.

8   See Madec, *Saint Augustin et la philosophie*, 18–19.

had "absolutized" the two and set them up in ontological opposition to each other: matter against spirit, and equivalently, evil against good. Augustine, rather, distinguished two kinds of being within a single hierarchy of being.[9] He had always known that the world he perceived with his senses existed outside of his mind. He came to understand that the intelligible "world" existed only within his mind and that he could understand the latter only insofar as it was "located" there. He eventually grasped that the intelligible world is "where" it is and what it is, because, precisely, its presence to the mind is not mediated by the senses of the body. Although the intelligible world is within us (and even God as intelligible, for that matter), Augustine also understood that the sensible world cannot even be perceived except through the interiority of our memory. The sensible, material world is not antagonistic to spirit; it is the spiritual, intelligible world that relates to the existence of the sensible.

The first category of things stored in our memory consists of those products of sense perception[10] which Saint Augustine catalogued among the *sensibilia*, sensed realities. Our coming to know anything about the world beyond ourselves happens through sense perception. Whatever we know as being in the corporeal, spatial, temporal continua of the world outside of ourselves, "out there," we come to know, as "bodily" knowledge, by exercising our five senses. There may exist far more things external to our perception that we will never know about, because we do not have any other sense besides our five by which to perceive them.

Augustine always stressed that sense perception is a reciprocal

---

9 Augustine may have depended upon Porphyry for his formulation of the idea of the "degrees of being." According to the latter, the "beings" within the universe are lined up according to their forms along the axis between Supreme Being and non-being. Profiting always from two different traditions, the Platonic and the Biblical, Augustine assimilated what he learned from Porphyry to the doctrine of creation. See G. Madec, *Petites études augustiniennes* (Paris: 1994), 138–9.

10 O'Daly, 80–105.

process by which the will engages the senses to perceive spatiotemporal realities and by which the senses reflect back to the memory
the images of those realities. "Image-ination" is that instantaneous
process by which the continua of the world perceived are transformed into images that the memory stores within itself. The images are not themselves the things perceived but the likenesses of
the things perceived. Sense perception is an active process by which
imagination de-materializes and de-temporalizes the things out
there and transforms them into dimensionless and timeless images
that we internalize into an infinite number of stored images. Subsequently recalling those internal images replaces the role of their
original image-ination through sense perception (*Trin.* 11.3,6–
7,11).[11]

The likenesses stored in our memories are reductions of spatiotemporal continua into an infinite number of memory fragments.
These can never amount to the full continua of spatiotemporal realities, because our attention to one aspect of a continuum is simultaneously a distraction away from others. Sense perception is
not a matter of passively receiving "vibes" from the world out
there, because sensing anything is first of all a matter of the will.
Does it not happen to us, even several times a day, not to have
heard something quite audible when we were being attentive to
something else? Waiting for that important phone call you never
heard the dog whimpering in his sleep. Does it not happen to us
not to have seen something obvious, because we were looking for
something else? I never saw the can of tuna because I was looking
for the light blue label. Whatever we perceive out there is a matter
of intentionality, which is within us.

Spatiotemporal reality is too vast and too extensive for us to
be able to grasp in its entirety. Perceiving anything is itself an act
of the memory. We cannot grasp what another is saying without
having committed to memory the beginning even of a sentence to
reach its full meaning by the end of it (11:15,20). We cannot appreciate a mountain-scape without having committed to memory

11 Howells, 218.

our first glance at it which has subsequently become peripheral to a second look. The complete picture lies only in our memory. Actually, all we know of the world outside of ourselves is the conglomerate of likenesses each of which we had stored instantaneously into our memories during the still-point of the present. Sense perception, for all its dependence upon physiological conditions,[12] is over and above a psychological process (*Trin.* 11:7,11).[13]

The images we have of the world within our memories are not the world itself but remembered likenesses stored as fragments in the serial succession by which they were stored there. Augustine identified that kind of remembering as the acquisition of *fantasiae*. At first blush our reproductive memory of reality as we individually perceive it can seem to be a vast reduction and impoverishment from the spatiotemporal world which we can never grasp in its near infinite wholeness. Our memory, however, can do far more than just remember those likenesses in the serial order in which they were remembered through the medium of sense perception.

Imagination

A second category of things shelved in the memory, also as *sensibilia*, are produced by a constructive, creative imagination (10:8,12; *Trin.* 11:8,12),[14] which can extract memory's images from the temporal serial experiences by which they were perceived and conceived subsequently as discrete memory fragments. The creative imagination can then recombine those memory bits into internal realities that are not likenesses of spatiotemporal realities but figments of the creative imagination, what Augustine labeled *phantasmata*.[15] We can conceive things which do not exist externally

12 O'Daly, 80–84.
13 O'Daly, 84–87.
14 O.Daly, 106–130.
15 Augustine's distinction between *fantasia* and *phantasma* can be found for example in *On Music* 6:32 and *Trin.* 8:6,9; 9:6,10.

but which begin to exist only within our memories and will hence always be present there. Everyone knows what a unicorn looks like, but no one has ever seen one cantering in an external wood. We are able to put a unicorn together from the myriad images supplied in our memories, and when the unicorn is born it will then always be present in our memories.

While residing only within the storehouse of memory, the phantasms are no less real than the fantasies of external spatiotemporal realities. Our connection to spatiotemporal continua is itself mediated through their likenesses which reside within the same internal library that stores our phantasms. Our experience of the external world is just as internal and individual as are the things produced by our creative imagination. Conversely, our phantasms are just as real as are our fantasies. The macrocosm we had thought as existing externally to us turns out to be the microcosm when compared to the greater macrocosm within our memory (10:8,14; 17,26), a macrocosm peopled also with giants and dwarfs, ents and centaurs, cherubim and men from Mars, a macrocosm teeming with unicorns and prophetic asses, lions lying with lambs, talking snakes and foolish pigs, a macrocosm where burning bushes grow and water forms walls of safe passage and prophets disappear in chariots of fire.

Augustine's perception of any external event was a matter of the event slipping through the still-point of the present, when it became a *fantasia* of his memory. Ultimately, both fantasies and phantasms are internal realities, existing within the memory. Since both are matters of the memory, Augustine's understanding of the "literal meaning" of, say, an event narrated in the Scriptures, is different from what we ordinarily think of as the literal meaning. What happens "literally," in our ordinary sense of the word, is something that is perceived actually in the form of image, of fantasy in the memory. Since perception and creative "image-ination" are active activities of the mind, both perceived *fantasiae* and creatively imagined *phantasmata* are realities existing in the memory. Elizabeth Barrett Browning's poem, taken from *Sonnets from the Portuguese* sums it up very nicely:

Earth's crammed with heaven,
And every common bush afire with God;
But only he who sees, takes off this shoes,
The rest sit round it and pluck blackberries,
And daub their natural faces unaware.

Moses saw the burning bush; nobody else would have seen the blackberry bush afire. The same bush; two very different "events." The meaning of either is actually the event itself!

The Intelligibles

Now for that third category of things remembered in our memory: the *intelligibilia*. They prevent those things perceived as well as those creatively imagined from constituting a solipsistic reality that would be purely subjective for being dependent upon personal experience and creative imagination. The things of this category never enter the memory through the imaging of sense perception. They are always there; we have never learned them through our will's "bodily" interaction with the world external to our individual selves; and we know them only by remembering them whenever we inevitably evaluate anything within our memory as being good or evil, true or false, beautiful or ugly (10:10,17).[16] The *intelligibilia*, which all human beings can experience in common, are characteristic of the soul.[17] We know them "spiritually."

The good, the true and the beautiful are not objects of our knowing directly, as are the remembered objects of sense perception or of

---

16 Augustine, in *Mag.* 14,45, had previously explained that a teacher does not transmit his knowledge to his disciple, but can only elicit within him his own inner discovery of the immutable "transcendentals" that leads him toward the apprehension of Truth.

17 Would the *intelligibilia*, which we all experience in common within our memories, indicate ultimately that we all participate in one "world-soul?" Augustine was never able to decide and remained agnostic on this issue. See: O'Daly, 7–79; Teske, "The World-Soul and Time in St. Augustine," *Augustinian Studies* 14 (1983): 75–92.

constructive imagination. Rather, they emerge into our awareness by indirection, within the relationship between the mind knowing and the object known. We become aware of them as if by triangulation, based on the direct line between the two fixed points of knower and known. They are referred to as the "transcendentals," because the awareness of them cannot be pursued as are the objects of our knowing. They are like light, invisible in itself, by which we see everything seen. The good, the true, and the beautiful cannot be objects of our intellectual endeavor; they happen to us, rather, within the binary relationship between us as knowers and the objects of our knowing. Our consciousness of the transcendentals emerges indirectly when we can relate to the objects of our knowing in terms of their endemic value. Knowing the *intelligibilia* indirectly is not like possessing the objective knowledge of separate and substantial realities; it is being possessed by participation in the value of those objects.[18] The objects of our knowing are the medium through which the transcendentals are experienced, not willfully but gratuitously.

Knowing the *sensibilia* is by way of "bodily" knowledge. Experiencing the *intelligibilia* is by way of a "spiritual" coincidental relationship to the objects of our knowing. The difference between knowing the sensibles directly and perceiving the intelligibles indirectly marks the difference also between knowledge and wisdom, knowing (*sciens*) and enjoying (*sapiens*). In a remarkable little autobiography, *Surprised by Joy*, C.S. Lewis describes joy as what could happen to him as he engaged himself, even as a boy, in reading. It would happen by surprise, longed for but impossible to "be gotten again," slipping away as soon as it was noticed, making any intellectual enterprise infinitely worthwhile while fending off all endeavor, ungraspable but totally enthralling, usually present by its absence, grief its common counterpart.[19] The good, the true and

18 I am especially beholden to Howells, especially at 209f. He cites *Trin.* 1:1,1; 8:6–7,10; 9:3,3; 9:6,10–11; 10:5,7–8; 13:5,8.
19 C.S. Lewis, *Surprised by Joy* (New York: 1955), especially 17–18, 34–35, 71–78, 118–119, 130, 165–181, 217–221.

the beautiful, like joy, can never be grasped; they can be experienced only by indirection. Wisdom is living, longing for the transcendentals, the possible byproducts of all knowing.

The *intelligibilia* are not only the innate, but corollary, criteria by which we can distinguish the good, the true, and the beautiful and judge the measure by which any reality participates in any of them. They also provide us with the principles of conduct as well as those by which abstractions from the reproductive and creative memory emerge into concepts and into the arts and sciences (10:9,16).[20] These become obvious when the intelligibles cluster around themselves the *fantasiae* and *phantasmata* of the memory. The sciences are concerned with matters knowable and they emerge from within the memories of people like Plato, Aristotle, Thomas Aquinas, Heisenberg, and Einstein, who dwelt in their memories, where they could combine the intelligibles with their store of images and phantasms. The arts are concerned with things do-able and they emerge from within the memories of people like Shakespeare, Hildegard von Bingen, Clara Schumann, and Georges Rouault, who dwelt in their memories, where they also could combine the intelligibles with their store of images and phantasms.

Memory is the meeting place with other humans (10:8,14).[21] It goes without saying that language is fundamental to human encounter.[22] But Augustine specifically constructed his ideal of community life from associations treasured in his memory (4:11,17). Some have criticized Augustine's trinitarian accounts of the human person in his *The Trinity*, as being too individualistic.[23] That Augustine had wanted to write the *Confessions* belies that view. Intellectual friendships are built from individual reproductive and constructive experiences which can be shared, but only because of

20 O'Daly, 107–114.
21 Wills, 18–22.
22 O'Daly, 24–25; 28–29; 114; 134–135; 141–147; 155–157; 160; 171–178.
23 See for instance: C. LaCugna, *God for Us: The Trinity and Christian Life* (San Francisco: 1991), 91–101.

the *intelligibilia* which are held in common from the same soul-source. The arts and sciences evolve from memory shared. National cultures grow out of memory. It is through memory that we of the twenty-first century can communicate with the men and women of past millennia. We all become contemporaries through the present of the past. The dead through memory become current interlocutors.

Memory is not only the crossroad where men and women of all times meet one another. It is also is the crucible in which time and space coalesce into one reality. Our perceiving things and "imaging" them, transforming them from being material, spatial, temporal things (10:8,12) into spiritual things, is the only process, the only thing that happens in the still-point of time That is the only thing that happens when what is not yet slips through the present into what is no longer. Augustine is more precise: what is no longer, is no longer out there; it continues to be, within the presence of our memory (10:8,13). The world which we think of as being external to us is the small world contained within the instant immediacy of sense perception and its attendant "imaging." In fact, when we speak of the universe, we are actually not speaking of the universe out there, but of the universe that we have internalized and filed away within our memories (10:8,12). The sky is out there and our modern telescopes, though able to peer deeply into fields of stars, provide us with only a reductionist view of our sky. The object of astronomy, however, is in our memory (Cf. 10:10,17).

On another note, we usually conceive of ourselves as existing in the present. So long as we do that, we entertain very narrow concepts of ourselves, because the present is that fleeting still-point when what we see, hear, touch, taste or smell slips into the past. Saint Augustine discovered for himself that it is far more gratifying to dwell in his memory. Life in the present is too fleeting. It lasts for as long as it takes for the future to slip into the past: not even as long as a nano-second. Life lived in the present lasts as long as it takes sense perceptions to dematerialize the world perceived into images kept within the memory. Augustine could have wallowed in the depressing thought that time flashes by so fast we find ourselves dying before we can begin to live. Augustine decided not to live in the future, which does not yet exist. And he shied away from living in the present, because the present is nothing other than the future's slippage into the past.

Saint Augustine, rather, chose to live within his memory,[24] where the present gives way to the presence of things remembered. He left the present behind to become present to himself within his memory (10:8,14). He discovered that human existence there lasts a lifetime, rather than through the extent of a fleeting flash point. The *Confessions* limns Augustine's springing to life by becoming aware of himself within his memory. Augustine remembering himself was more real than Augustine having lived in the vaporizing present. As he remembered his individual experiences, he found himself combining those experiences into clusters that had not existed when he experienced them in the singularity of what had been their present. Within the creative imagination of his memory, he was becoming more human than was the man who had originally experienced his temporal experiences. Some people will fault Saint Augustine for presenting them with a man different from the one they discovered when they had read the writings that antedated the *Confessions*. What Augustine was intending to do, however, was to reveal the Augustine who was discovering himself by remembering within the memory of his mind (10:8,14; also 14,21 and 17,26). His *Confessions* represents a second conversion[25] that propelled him into an episcopal ministry that has provided one of the underpinnings of the Christian west.

As he was discovering the intelligibles within his memory, by which he could perceive the good, the true and the beautiful, he was allowing himself to be discovered by their very source within himself: everlasting Goodness that is God, the Truth himself, and Beauty ever ancient, ever new (10:27,38). As he delved into his

---

24 O'Daly, 148–150.

25 O'Donnell, *Augustine: Confessions*, vol. 1 (Oxford University Press, New York: 1992), xlv–xlvii.

memory, he was discovering the ever deepening, ultimately unfathomable, depths of himself (10:8,15)[26] and, therein by indirection, the God (10:20,29) who was more within him than his own inmost self and the God who transcended him (10:17,26; 26,37) beyond his highest self (3:6,11).[27] It was within the more real world of his memory that he found himself and God (10:24,35) enwrapped together within the same reality.[28]

The Scriptures became the story of Augustine remembering himself within his memory. All the wonders narrated in their stories were just as real as the Augustine he was finding in his remembering. And his creative remembering was spinning out the story of himself by which the Biblical story took on a meaning more real than its literal interpretation. Conversely, he was discovering that the literal meaning of the Scriptures became just as real as the story of himself that he was recounting by his remembering. And thereby the literal meaning of the Scriptures was becoming the allegory of Augustine's existence within his memory. That explains how the *Confessions* are from beginning to end a prayer addressed to God,[29] woven together with the words of Scripture[30] which became Divine Revelation for Augustine. Adam and Eve, Abraham and Sarah, Moses, Elijah and Ezekiel, Jesus and Paul, all were his contemporaries within his memory. In the final analysis, Saint Augustine was describing and formulating the consciousness of his personal identity in terms of his awareness of God's presence within his memory (10:24,35).[31]

Memory was the center of Saint Augustine's identity (10:8,14). We are what we remember. We remember reproductively what we

---

26 Solignac, "La mémoire selon saint Augustin," *BA* 14, 559–560: Wills, 11–14.
27 See G. Madec, *Le Dieu d'Augustin* (Paris: 2000).
28 Wills, 22–26.
29 Wills, xii.
30 Solignac, "Le jeu de vocabulaire et son sens dans les *Confessions* (I,i,1)," *BA* 13, 647–650.
31 Solignac, "La mémoire selon saint Augustin," *BA* 14, 564–566.

perceived of the world out there. We perceived what we willed to perceive; we do not remember what we decided not to perceive; and our memory contains all the images of everything we had willed to perceive. Additionally, we remember what we imagined creatively. What we imagined creatively through endless combinations of discrete images constitutes a macrocosmic inner world more fantastic that the universe we perceived as existing outside of ourselves. This inner world, in its infinite limitlessness, is the beginning of everlasting life that transcends the still-point of the present moment. We remember indirectly also the spiritual realities by which we judge everything else that we remember in our memory as being good, or true, or beautiful. If Augustine were alive today, he would see memory like a laboratory, "in which we are [constantly] refashioning everything we remember–which is everything we know. We even remake ourselves in that crucible."[32]

It is also important to remember that our future actions are conceived in the womb of memory. Things remembered are not disjointed, fragmented bytes of memory, but chains of past consequences, whose trajectories we can project into the future (10:8,14).[33] To the extent that we learn and live by all that we remember within our memory, whether always treasured, whether subsequently disapproved (10:14,21) or whether expectantly feared, we are on the path to the holiness that transcends whatever time is.

Book Ten of Augustine's *Confessions* is the hinge between the account of God's search for Augustine (10:27,38) over the course of Books One through Nine, prior to his baptism, and a meditation on God's Trinity through the concluding three Books, the Trinity into which he had been baptized. This hinge pivots on its still-point, from Augustine's re-presentation of his spatiotemporal experience, turning toward eternal Being that exists nowhere, beyond space and time. Book Ten, with its concentration on memory, tells us

32 Wills, 11.
33 Wills, 14–18.

what Augustine thought he had been doing with Books One through Nine. Memory was important not only because he was remembering his life. Memory was the place where he met himself, everybody else, and God.[34]

Above the Intelligibles

When we happen to discover the intelligibles within our memory of things knowable, we are also remembering an *a priori* "super-intelligible," the principle by which we can distinguish one *intelligibilium* from the other two, by which we know that none is reducible to another, and by which we sense innately the specific difference among them (Cf. 10:11,18). Incidentally, the difference between the "one" and the three *intelligibilia* helps by way of analogy to grasp the difference between the unity of God and God's trinity.

As Augustine remembered who he was becoming, he discovered for himself that he, like any of us, was being created in the image of God.[35] As *imago dei*, Augustine found within himself images of the Trinity.[36] Remembering, knowing, and willing are three specific aspects of the inwardness of a human being (*Trin.* 10). Each is irreducible to the other two, and all three are equal because the are united by the substance of one mind. As *imago dei*, the human mind is a triadic substance (*Sermon* 398,2), constituted of remembering, knowing and willing. There are three "presents" within the memory: the present of the past, by which we re-construct ourselves, is the analogue within us of God the Father, creating the universe;[37] the present of the present, by which we understand ourselves, is the analogue within us of the Word who expresses the passage of eternity into time and mediates God to us; and the present of the future, by which we project ourselves out of the past, is the analogue of the

---

34 Solignac, *BA* 14, 564–566; Wills, xi.
35 " . . . You have made us and drawn us to yourself, and our heart is unquiet until it rests inn you" (1:1,1).
36 Madec, *Saint Augustin et la philosophie*, 107–114.
37 Wills, xi.

Holy Spirit, who completes the mission of the Word-made-Flesh by conveying us back to the Father (*Trin.* 10:11,18).[38]

Like Augustine inaugurating his episcopal ministry by remembering his *Confessions*,[39] we can project a better future for ourselves to the extent that we dwell more deeply and extensively in our memory. The "once and future self" not only thrives within memory; it can there reach out to God the Future just as God the Past has been reaching out to it, also from within the memory.

38 Wills, 23–25.
39 J. J. O'Donnell, xlii–l.

Augustine's Confessions and Augustine's *Confessions: Ipsa est beata vita*
Daniel P. Maher

"This is the happy life, to rejoice over you, to you,
and because of you: this it is, and there is no other."
Confessions, Book X, Chapter 22[1]

Augustine's confessions are not simply identical to Augustine's *Confessions*. By writing, he transposes a hidden and unworldly activity into a physical thing accessible in the world. Through his editorial labors Augustine depicts for our eyes to see man as a creature whose highest excellence is not philosophical contemplation, not moral and political activity, but the utterly novel activity of confession.

Confessions is driven by three events, none being evident except through the evidence of speech or writing and each enjoying priority in its own fashion: the choice to create, the choice to reveal, and Augustine's conversion. The events themselves never manage to appear; rather, speech or writing concerning them is taken up with the significance of their *having already occurred*. The meaning of

1   St. Augustine, *Confessions*, trans. by John K. Ryan (New York: Doubleday, 1960), 251; *et ipsa est beata vita, gaudere de te, ad te, propter te: ipsa est et non est altera*. For the Latin text I have used the Loeb Classical Library edition: *St. Augustine's* Confessions, 2 volumes, translated by W. Watts, (Cambridge, Mass.: Harvard University Press, 1977 and 1979). (Subsequent references to Augustine's text will be identified parenthetically by book and chapter in the body of this essay.)

these events in Augustine's life is confessed and published as paradigmatic for all.

I. The Revealed Choice to Create[2]

By choosing to create "things that are not what you are but yet exist" (XII.11) God freely departs from eternal solitude; his enduring separation from created natures, in whose company he does not fit, as it were, is overcome only through choosing to reveal what was always true, but never before seen. God uncovers for the world himself as creator and itself as created. The hiddenness of God and of the fact of creation from the world itself mirrors the eternal solitude and self-sufficiency of the God who could be alone, neither appearing to nor lying hidden from any other: "For there is none other with you" (IX.4). Choosing to reveal lays bare both God and the fact of creation as now accessible to the world.

What God thus uncovers, that "In the beginning God made the heavens and the earth" (Gen. 1:1), is an unheard of way to think about the world. Pagan thinking (the natural, human articulation of the whole) takes the whole as final and fundamental, the eternal and necessary context within which all of the kinds or parts, including the divine, find their place in distinction from one another. Authentically pagan gods are always gods *of the world*; there is never a sense in which they could simply be and be all that they are without a world for which they are the gods. In contrast, Augustine confesses that God is the creator by choice, not by nature. "Needful of no good," (XIII.38) "you created heaven and earth out of nothing" (XII.7).

> Therefore what would be wanting in you for that good which you yourself are for yourself, even if none of these

2   This section draws heavily upon the sense of God articulated by Thomas Prufer, in "Notes for a Reading of Augustine, *Confessions*, Book X," *Interpretation* 10 (1982): 197–200, and by Robert Sokolowski, especially in *The God of Faith and Reason*, (Notre Dame, Ind.: University of Notre Dame Press, 1982).

things existed in any way or remained without form?
These things you have made, not out of any need, but
out of the fullness of your goodness, restraining them
and converting them to a form, although not as if your
joy were to be fulfilled by them . . . not as if you had
been imperfect and were to be made perfect by their perfection. (XIII.4)[3]

God would be all that God is without ever becoming creator: the
divine nature is not constituted in distinction from any created nature nor even from the whole of creation. God, who might never
have been creator, is intelligible, to himself at least, solely in terms
of himself, through himself, apart from any foil against which he
might be contrasted. God is not one of the kinds of being: He has
no profile since there is no background against which he appears.

Whether or not this understanding of the world could have
been reached by human beings independently of revelation, in fact
no one did reach it.[4] God's own speech about God and the world

3   "Your creation subsists out of the fullness of your goodness, to the
    end that a good that would profit you nothing . . . would nevertheless
    not be non-existent, since it could be made by you. What claim on
    you had heaven and earth, which you made in the beginning?" Cf.
    XI.4: "You, therefore, O Lord, who are beautiful, made these things,
    for they are beautiful; you who are good made them, for they are
    good; you who are made them, for they are. Yet they are not so good,
    nor are they so beautiful as you, nor do they even be in such wise as
    you, their creator. Compared to you, they are neither good, nor beau-
    tiful, nor real. We know all this, thanks be to you, but our knowledge
    compared to your knowledge is ignorance" (XIII.2). This does not
    deny the goodness of created natures; it emphasizes the unworldly
    goodness that is God.
4   "I did not know either what must be thought concerning your sub-
    stantial being or what way led up to you or back to you. Therefore,
    since we were too weak to find the truth by pure reason, and for that
    cause we needed the authority of Holy Writ, I now began to believe
    that in no wise would you have given such surpassing authority

reveals the peculiar characteristic of the world: it naturally presents itself as eternal and necessary, the ultimate context within which all beings (including the divine) are to be understood, while, according to revelation, the world might never have been at all. The appearance in the world of the deepest truth about the world— namely, that it is not world (eternal, necessary, and including the divine as a part) but is creation (freely chosen by God and chosen to be such as it is)—necessitates radical re-reflection on the world-as-creation and the divine-as-creator. Augustine engages in this re-reflection anthropocentrically. That is, Augustine's re-reflection deliberately adopts the perspective of man as the decisive participant for the sake of whom the gulf between God and creation has been revealed. Creation's limit—its separation from God—is not exactly a part of creation, but, through the revelation that is for man, a glimpse of creation's limit appears and this opens a new, previously unimagined perspective on human life.

II. Conversion

Augustine's account of his own confrontation with Christian revelation incorporates the victory of that revelation over his pagan ways of thinking and acting. The temporal priority of the pagan over the Christian sets the stage for conversion in the dramatic sense of renunciation of an embraced way of life, the sense of which life has been undone by a newly accepted truth.

Augustine's embraced way of life—"turned away from you, the One, I spent myself upon the many" (II.1)—stood in direct opposition to the Christian way of life. He resisted that way because the crudity of biblical expression concealed its inner meaning from him (III.5). He endorsed such teachings as appeared wise (III.6, ff.) and offered impunity from his shameful deeds (V.10). His conversion began when he perceived the defensibility of certain passages of

> throughout the whole world to that Scripture, unless you wished that both through it you be believed in and through it you be sought" (VI.5).

Scripture (V.11 and V.14), though, "while the Catholic position did not seem to be overthrown, neither did it appear to be the victor" (V.14). Such indecision contributed to affiliation with the skeptical Academics (V.10 and V.14): "I doubted everything and wavered in the midst of all things."

A. Understanding God

> The decisive question concerned the nature of God: I wished to meditate upon my God, but I did not know how to think of him except as a vast corporeal mass, for I thought that anything not a body was nothing whatsoever. This was the greatest and almost the sole cause of my inevitable error.
>
> As a result, I believed that evil is some such substance and that it possesses its own foul and hideous mass. . . . I postulated two masses opposed to one another, each of them infinite, but the evil one on a narrower scale, the good one larger. (V.10)

Emphatic assertion of the incorruptibility of God (though still conceived as corporeal, "because I could think of nothing different" (VII.1)) led him to reject this Manichean view. For truly immutable and inviolable divine nature is not susceptible to the postulated eternal contention with an evil nature (VII.2).[5] The undoing of Manichean dualism left him with "no explicit and orderly knowledge of the origin of evil" (VII.3) and its status in the world.

Uncertain and searching, Augustine was led along a "way of humility" (VII.9), which included the rejection of the vain thoughts of those "Platonists" who professed wisdom yet failed to attain the fullness of truth as revealed by God. They "'changed the truth of God into a lie; and worshipped and served the creature rather than

---

5   This refutation of eternal (substantial) evil is not Christian insofar as it embraces a pagan understanding of God. At VII.12 he rejects the doctrine of substantial evil on Christian terms.

the Creator' (Rom. 1:25)" (VII.9). Thus, Scripture's rejection of pagan idolatry admonished him to return to himself, and immediately Augustine entered into his inmost being and saw there an unchangeable light, not the light plain to all flesh, but a light different from all other lights (VII.10). This light was above his mind, not spatially (i.e., corporeally), but *because it made him* (VII.10).[6]

> I beheld other things below you, and I saw that they are not altogether existent nor altogether non-existent: they are, because they are from you; they are not, since they are not what you are. For that truly exists which endures unchangeably. (VII.11)

The understanding of God as creator in the (Christian) unworldly sense becomes plain to Augustine in light of the revealed, scriptural rejection of the (pagan) worldly estimation of God. Recognition that God does not fit alongside or among the kinds within the world (because he made them) sets God at a Christian distance from the world. Seeing God as creator and world as created opens the door to the Christian refutation of substantial evil.

> But evil, of which I asked 'Whence is it?' is not a substance, for if it were a substance, it would be good. Either it would be an incorruptible substance, a great good indeed, or it would be a corruptible substance, and it would not be corruptible unless it were good. Hence I saw and it was made manifest to me that you have made all things good, and that there are no substances whatsoever that you have not made. (VII.12)

6   Cf. VII.15: "I looked back over other things, and I saw that they owe their being to you, and that all finite things are in you. They are there, not as though in a place, but in a different fashion, because you contain all things in your hand by your truth." Such Christian descriptions of God are contrary to emphatically bodily conceptions of God in VII.5 and VII.14.

This is a formulation of the doctrine of creation. God alone is eternal (VII.15) and chose that creation be and be good, not evil. This non-Manichean view expresses the mastery of God over creation: "To you, nothing whatsoever is evil, and not only to you but also to your whole creation, for outside of it there is nothing that can break in and disrupt the order that you have imposed upon it" (VII.13). Evil is a worldly phenomenon, or, better, it depends upon there being a world, and Augustine seeks evil's origin among creation's parts (VII.13).

B. Understanding Evil

God has created all things good in themselves and, objectively, "All things are in harmony not only with their proper places, but also with their seasons" (VII.15). Consequently, "There is no health in them to whom any part of your creation is displeasing" (VII.14). The judgment that some part of creation is evil reveals a sickness in the one making the judgment. That sickness is the root of evil.

> It is no strange thing that the bread that pleases a healthy appetite is offensive to one that is not healthy, and that light is hateful to sick eyes, but welcome to the well. Your justice offends the wicked (*iniqui*). . . .
>
> I asked, 'What is iniquity?' and I found that it is not a substance. It is perversity of will, twisted away from the supreme substance, yourself, O God, and towards lower things, and casting away its own bowels, and swelling beyond itself. (VII.16)[7]

7   Also: "The only thing that does not come from you is what does not exist, together with any movement of the will away from you who are and towards that which is in a lesser way, for such movement is crime and sin" (XII.11); "With you our good lives forever, and because we have turned away from you, we have become perverted" (IV.16)

Inquiry into the sickness (iniquity) that judges God's justice to be evil explains evil. The doctrine of creation founds and shapes a doctrine of iniquity (or moral evil): there is a created part of man that is directed outside of creation to the creator; iniquity is perversion of this unworldly relationship. The relationship[8] itself obtains between God and man by virtue of creation. For, first of all, the doctrine of creation includes the teaching, "You have made us for yourself" (I.1), "nor have you fashioned me to seek after those many other things, which are not what you are" (IX.4).[9] In other words, the doctrine of creation implies a moral doctrine of continence: "You enjoin continence. . . . By continence we are gathered together and brought back to the One, from whom we have dissipated our being into many things" (X.29; cf. III.8).

The re-orientation of man, a part of God's creation (I.1)—*away* from the many things that are not what God is but yet exist (XII.11) and *toward* him, the one who made them but is not one among them, *away* from "that disordered state in which I lay in shattered pieces" (II.1), *toward* the one who "gathers me together again" (II.1)—is the natural extension of the unnatural doctrine of creation. The creation doctrine founds a doctrine of continence, iniquity, and conversion.

Continence, iniquity, and conversion cannot be understood exclusively within creation's limits. Their being understood depends upon the revealed understanding of God as not a part of the world. They specify the relation that obtains between a God who is not in the world and a part of man that of itself never appears in the world among men. Moral good and evil, or continence and iniquity, are constituted in the relation bearing between the will and

8   "For in truth society itself, which must obtain between God and us, is violated, when the nature of which he is author is polluted by a perverted lust. . . . Every part that is not in harmony with its whole is a vile thing" (III.8).

9   See also XIII.8: "You sufficiently reveal how great you made the rational creature. For in no wise is any being less than you sufficient to give it rest and happiness, and for this it is not sufficient to itself."

God more so than in the speeches and deeds of men and between men in the world. The iniquity of the evil deed lies especially in the perversity of the will from which it arises, and the goodness of the good deed lies principally in the uprightness of the will. To say this does not yet relocate moral goodness to some other world and thereby despoil human action of its moral character. Rather, Augustine roots the moral elements of human activities and relationships within the world in something more fundamental than the world itself.[10]

This relation between the will and God is hidden within and invisible to all except a man himself, who speaks, as does Augustine throughout *Confessions*,[11] "in your presence, by myself and to

10 A rightly ordered will leads to continent deeds and deeds of profligacy issue from a disordered will. Augustine says nothing to suggest that, say, fornication may be good if it springs from a rightly ordered will. Rather, an act of fornication only springs from a will not governed by continence. "For in truth society itself, which must obtain between God and us, is violated, when the nature of which he is author is polluted by a perverted lust" (III.8). Fornication is bad itself and chastity good, but their primary badness and goodness originate not in the visible, worldly nature of the act, but in the more fundamental relation between God and the will in its willing. "Love (*amicitia*) of this world is fornication against you" (I.13; cf. *Letter of James* 4:4). "Thus the soul commits fornication [metaphorically] when it is turned away from you and, apart from you, seeks such pure, clean things as it does not find except when it returns to you" (II.6). Acts of chastity externally express a continent state of the will, its being gathered together and directed toward the One, away from the many. "By command of you, its Lord God, our soul germinates works of mercy according to its kind. For that it loves its neighbor is shown in the relief of bodily necessities, and it has seed in itself according to its likeness" (XIII.17). Cf. II.6; IV.2; IX.8; XIII.26–7.

11 Confessions are made in solitude by one who has returned to himself and entered into his inmost being (VII.10), not "with bodily words and sounds but with words uttered by the soul and with outcry of thought, of which your ear has knowledge" (X.2). By contrast, *Con-*

myself out of the closest feelings of my mind" (IX.4), "close to my heart, where I am whatever I am" (X.3). This moral privacy appears most strikingly in Augustine's confession of the event of his conversion.

C. Conversion of Will

Knowledge of the need for conversion was secure before the conversion itself was achieved: "I had now found the good pearl, and this I must buy, after selling all that I had. Yet still I hesitated" (VIII.1).[12] Hesitation arises from the strength of voluntary habit: "The enemy had control of my will, and out of it he fashioned a chain and fettered me with it. For in truth lust is made out of a perverse will, and when lust is served it becomes habit, and when habit is not resisted, it becomes necessity" (VIII.5). The evil of the deeds done, even out of habit, is traced to the perversity of the will that is their source. Iniquity is the perverse orientation of the will toward the world, toward the things that are not God. Its pure state is to be oriented away from the world and toward its creator. Conversion, then, requires that the will re-orient itself. It is an internal struggle, an interior accomplishment, achieved through no visible, exterior action whatsoever.

---

fessions is written "not only before you (*coram te*) in secret exultation with trembling and in secret sorrow with hope, but also in the ears of believing sons of men" (X.4).

12 "Your words had stuck fast in the depths of my heart, and on every side I was encompassed by you. I was now certain that you are eternal life, although I saw it only 'in a glass, in a dark manner' (I Cor. 13:12). Yet all my doubts concerning incorruptible substance, and that every other substance comes from it, had been removed from me. It was not to be more certain concerning you, but to be more steadfast in you that I desired. But in my temporal life all things were uncertain, and my heart had to be cleansed of the old leaven. The way, the Savior himself, had become pleasing, but as yet I was loath to tread its narrow passes" (VIII.1).

I did not enter into your will and into a covenant with you, my God. . . . Not by ships, or in chariots, or on foot do we enter therein; we need not go even so far as I had gone from the house to the place where we were sitting. For not only to go, but even to go in thither was naught else but the will to go, to will firmly and finally, and not to turn and toss, now here, now there, a struggling, half-maimed will, with one part rising upwards and another falling down. (VIII.8)

Augustine exploits the bodily manifestation of his emotional and spiritual torment to emphasize the difference between willing and acting. Bodily movements require not only a willing, but also the ability to act (VIII.8). Conversion is not external action; it is a motion of the will itself.

In such an act the power to act and the will itself are the same, and the very act of willing is actually to do the deed. Yet it was not done: it was easier for the body to obey the soul's most feeble command, so that its members were moved at pleasure, than for the soul to obey itself and to accomplish its own high will wholly within the will. (VIII.8)[13]

The act of conversion is solitary and private in a way unlike external actions. It is not visible. It is not achieved through the body or through spoken words. It is not something directly accessible to men who live in common.[14] When Augustine finally manages to

13 Ponticianus relates a conversion story in which an unnamed man says, "But to become God's friend, if I wish it (*si voluero*), see, I become one here and now" (VIII.6).

14 For this reason even the spiritual man is a doer of the law and not a judge: "Nor does he judge concerning that distinction, namely, of spiritual and carnal men, who are known to your eyes, O our God, but have not yet become apparent to us by their works, so that we

will with efficacy, he is, without surprise, reading,[15] silently, but not alone.

> So I hurried back to the spot where Alypius was sitting,
> for I had put there the volume of the apostle when I got

might know them by their fruits. But you, O Lord, already know them, and you have divided them apart, and you have called them in secret before the firmament was made" (XIII.23). "Between them and us, in this still uncertain state of man's knowledge, you alone distinguish, 'who prove our hearts' (I Thess. 2:4) and 'call the light day, and the darkness night.' (Gen. 1:5) For who discerns what we are but you?" XIII.14). Others do not know what a man is within himself, "where they can extend neither their eye nor ear nor mind" (X.3).

15 Reading occasions many conversions described in *Confessions*: Augustine and Alypius (VIII.12), Victorinus (VIII.2), Anthony (VIII.6), and the unnamed men described by Ponticianus (VIII.6), about one of whom Augustine or Ponticianus says, "He read on and was changed within himself, where your eye could see. His mind was stripped of this world, as soon became apparent." All this is consistent with the importance given to reading throughout *Confessions*. In III.12, Augustine recounts how Monica implored a learned bishop to refute Augustine's Manicheanism; the bishop told her, "He will find out by reading what is the character of that error and how great is its impiety." Reading, in the fashion of Ambrose (VI.3), draws one inward and has the effect of absenting the reader from his immediate surroundings. Reading the written word, like thinking and praying, is capable of absorbing a reader in such a manner that the world around falls away into irrelevancy (see especially VIII.6). This provocative theme is essential to understanding why Augustine transformed his confessions into his *Confessions*. Consider the extended account of reading Psalm 4 in the early days of his conversion (IX.4). Consider additionally that, for those who live "by faith and not yet by sight" (XIII.13), reading Scripture is analogous to reading the face of God for those in heaven who "always behold your face" (XIII.15). And Augustine turns the reading of the first few verses of *Genesis* into an interior dialogue occupying books XI–XIII: "your truth is not silent inwardly in my mind" (XII.16); cf. especially XII.11.

up and left him. I snatched it up, opened it, and read in
silence the chapter on which my eyes first fell: "Not in
rioting and drunkenness, not in chambering and impuri-
ties, not in strife and envying; but put you on the Lord
Jesus Christ, and make not provision for the flesh in its
concupiscences" (Rom. 13:13, 14). No further wished I
to read, nor was there need to do so. Instantly, in truth,
at the end of this sentence, as if before a peaceful light
streaming into my heart, all the dark shadows of doubt
fled away. (VIII.12)

Years of voluntary habit and anguished struggle are undone an-
ticlimactically in a moment. God works conversion in the heart,
but the specific nature of the event is obscure to the reader. What
did this reading achieve in Augustine that no other exhortation had
before achieved? What precisely did Augustine will "firmly and finally" (VIII.8) at that moment? Why does Augustine, who publicizes his privacies as a service to his brothers (X.4), suddenly
practice discretion? Given the tremendous insight of Augustine and
the need to bring hidden things to light (XI.1), it should not escape
notice that the dramatic climax of *Confessions* is left obscure. Silence at this juncture suggests that what is most essential to the relationship between God and the soul cannot be made to appear in
the world as it is in itself (cf. IX.4).

Augustine must tell Alypius what has happened within himself
and Alypius, in turn, tells what happened within himself. For
though each stood before the other when the events of conversion
occurred, this event is something of which only a man himself (at
most) can be witness. Conversion is not directly evident when it
occurs, nor after the fact, but is merely reportable through speech
or writing.[16]

16 "And with a countenance now calm, I told it all to Alypius (*indicavi
    Alypio*). What had taken place in him, which I did not know about,
    he then made known to me (*quod ego nesciebam—sic indicavit*)"
    (VIII.12). They went to Monica: "We told her the story, and she re-

D. Perfection

Conversion stops short of perfection. To be converted and continent is to be brought forth as a living soul (XIII.21; XIII.34). Beyond this a man "'is renewed unto knowledge of God, according to the image of him who created him' (Col. 3:10)" (XIII.22).

> When our affections have been restrained from love of this world, in which affections we were dying by living evilly, and when a living soul has begun to exist, and your Word, by which you spoke to us through your apostle, has been fulfilled in us, namely, 'Do not be conformed to this world,' there follows what you immediately adjoined, and said, 'But be reformed in the newness of your mind.' (Rom. 12:2) No longer is this 'after one's kind' as though imitating our neighbor who goes on before us, or living according to the example of some better man. . . .
>
> Therefore, you do not say, 'Let man be made,' but, 'Let us make man,' and you do not say, 'according to his kind,' but 'to our image and likeness.' For since he is renewed in mind and perceives your truth that he has understood, he does not need a man to point the way so that he may imitate his own kind. By your direction, he himself establishes what is your will, what is the good, and the acceptable, and the perfect thing. (XIII.22)

joiced. We related just how it happened (*indicamus: gaudet. narramus, quemadmodem gestum sit*)" (VIII.12). These events may be indicated or narrated but not perceived by others. The indirect evidence of the fact of conversion—outward deeds and speech—presents the possibility of hypocrisy (esp. X.1–4). See also the case of Victorinus, who wished to be a Christian by inward conviction rather than outward display; he responded to Simplicianus's criticisms by saying, "'Is it walls, then, that make men Christians?'" (VIII.2). Finally, consider the security in Monica's "unfeigned faith" (IX.12) coupled with the uncertainty caused by her sins (IX.13).

The perfection of man is not to be perfect in his kind, but to be perfect in the image or imitation of God. Man's conversion from his disordered state, or his being turned away from the many and directed toward the One who made him, is only the beginning. Man's perfection is something more, and it is not accessible to man as man; it is not by nature that man is directed to something outside the natural world. For while it remains true that "you have made us for yourself" (I.1), man's conversion and perfection depend upon God's choice to reveal. The possibility of conversion and perfection[17] is not open to man as man, but as one to whom the truth about God and the world has been revealed.

When the truth about God is revealed, the truth about man becomes obscure: "For in your sight I have become a riddle to myself, and that is my infirmity" (X.33).[18] The revelation of the fact of creation grounds a new understanding of human being

17 This is to be understood both in the sense of opportunity for conversion and perfection and in the sense of the capacity to be converted and perfected. Augustine asserts, "No man can be continent unless you grant it to him" (VI.11; cf. II.7; X.2; X.29). Similarly, perfection seems to depend upon the activity of God: "Power of my soul, enter into it and fit it for yourself, so that you may have it and hold it 'without spot or wrinkle' (Eph. 5:27)" (X.1).

18 Cf. X.5: "There is something further in man which not even that spirit of man which is in him knows. But you, Lord, who made him, know all things that are in him." At IX.1 Augustine asks, "Who am I, and what am I?" In Book X, where Augustine undertakes to confess "what I now am and what I still am" (X.4), he separates the who-question from the what-question, directing the first to himself (X.6) and the second to God (X.17), as if only God could tell him *what* he is: "Let me confess, then, what I know about myself. Let me confess also what I do not know about myself, since that too which I know about myself I know because you enlighten me. As to that which I am ignorant of concerning myself, I remain ignorant of it until my 'darkness shall be made as the noonday in your sight.' (Isa. 58:10)" (X.5). For this observation, see Hannah Arendt, *The Human Condition*, (Chicago: University of Chicago Press, 1958), 10–11.

and human excellence. God's not being a part of the world and man's being in the image of such a God suggests that God's apartness from the world is not finally prohibitive for man. Rather, man as abyss (IV.14, X.2, X.8, X.17), man as mind (X.6, X.7, X.16) represents a sort of perforation in creation, openness in an otherwise closed whole. The excellence of this being, made in the image of God, lies in the commerce between God and man at this point of contact, not in any worldly activity.[19] The perfection of man is a renewal of mind, deriving from the illuminating dialogue between God and man, the hidden activity of confession whereby God enlightens man's darkness and obscurity (IV.15; X.5).

IV. Publicity

Augustine claims not to know why Ambrose read silently; he read to refresh his mind, but the silence was mysterious (VI.3). Augustine hazards several possible and mundane conjectures, such as Ambrose's need to save his voice. Augustine could not understand what he saw; he could only guess at the invisible activity within Ambrose. In the next paragraph, Augustine says he did hear Ambrose's voice every Sunday "rightly handling the word of truth" (2 Tim. 2:15), and in what seems to be a change of subject, he says he

19 The superfluity of deeds parallels that of creation. Much as creation need not have been chosen without anything lacking in being, so deeds might never be done without anything lacking morally. The extreme formulation of this: "I say to you that every one who looks at a woman lustfully has already committed adultery with her in his heart" (Mt. 5:28). The integrity of deeds is not disparaged (X.4; XIII.21; XIII.38), just as created goods are not diminished but contextualized by knowledge of creation: "With regard to all these things, and others of like nature, sins are committed when, out of an immoderate liking for them, since they are the least goods, we desert the best and highest goods, which are you, O Lord our God, and your truth and your law. These lower goods have their delights, but none such as my God, who has made all things" (II.5).

learned that believers interpret spiritually the claim that "man was made by you to your image."

> But you, most high and most near at hand, most secret and most present, in whom there are no members, some greater and others smaller, who are everywhere whole and entire, who are never confined in place, and who surely are not in our corporeal shape, you have yet made man to your own image. And behold, from head to foot he is contained in space! (VI.3)

It is difficult to understand that within a man is a likeness to God and a nearness or openness or presence to God.[20] Augustine did not yet know how to understand what he heard (VI.4), which may explain why he could not understand what he saw Ambrose do. Ambrose's silence about his own silent reading left Augustine and his "carnal imagination" (VI.3) in the dark as to what lay within. He could not fathom what "spiritual substance" meant (VI.3), and he still thought unending bodily pleasure would satisfy a human being (VI.16). "Blind," he could not conceive the light that "is seen only from within (*ex intimo*)" (VI.16). The new conception of God, as the light that is somehow within and yet still above him because it made him (VII.10), entails a new conception of man, as made in the image and likeness of that God, and Augustine's *Confessions* trumpets his discovery of Christian interior life by publicizing his otherwise silent confessions.

At the outset, we said that *Confessions* turns on three events: the choice to create, the choice to reveal, and Augustine's conversion. We should add a fourth: the choice to write *Confessions*. This choice mimics God's choice to reveal, from which it is essentially derivative: the very words with which Augustine reveals himself

---

20 "I thought over these things and you were present to me (*aderas mihi*)" (VI.5). "I did not rest until you stood plain before my inner sight" (VII.8). "You are present, you who have created us" (*tu praesens, qui creasti*) (IX.8).

are borrowed and adapted from the words of Scripture, with which God reveals himself through salvation history.[21] Augustine *publicizes* his story of salvation in the form of his confession to God, which includes the confession of past sins but which reveals more directly his life today (X.3 and X.4). *Confessions* displays for our eyes to see what Augustine now is and how he sees today the sinner he once was and the path from there to here, all of which appears as the content of Augustine's *present* acts of confession to God. The man absorbed in confession turns his attention from God just enough to write his confessions down and thereby display for his brothers "what I am now, at this very time when I make my confessions" (X.3); his brothers believe him in charity (X.3) and love (*diligit*) him when they approve and rejoice in Augustine's good (accomplished through God's gift) and when they disapprove and are saddened by what is bad (X.4).

> May hymns and weeping ascend in your sight from the hearts of my brethren, your censers. . . .
> Such is the benefit from my confessions, not of what I have been, but of what I am, that I may confess this not only before you in secret exultation with trembling and in secret sorrow with hope, but also in the ears of believing sons of men, partakers of my joy and sharers in my mortality, my fellow citizens and pilgrims with me, those who go before me and those who follow me, and those who are companions on my journey. . . . Yet this your Word would be but little to me if he had given his precepts in speech alone and had not gone on before me by deeds. I do this service by deeds as well as by words. . . .
> Therefore, to such as you command me to serve I will

21 "Nor do I say any good thing to men except what you have first heard from me; nor do you hear any such thing from me but what you have first spoken to me" (X.2). "He who 'speaks a lie speaks of his own'" (John 8:44). Therefore, that I may speak the truth, I will speak out of your gift" (XIII.25).

reveal not what I have been but what I now am and what
I still am. (X.4)[22]

There are no deeds in *Confessions* except confessions to God and
the publication of those confessions. The words of his book would
mean much less without the deeds: without confession to God and
without publication for us. The benefit of the publicized confessions lies in the further confessions of his brothers or those who
become his brothers.

Augustine's openness before God runs deeper than his publicity
before others (X.5). It seems "sweet" to Augustine to confess *to*
God the inward changes worked in him by God when he was a
catechumen at Cassiciacum (IX.4). He confesses the wish that his
private reading of the psalms had been overheard (without Augustine's awareness) by the Manicheans, concerning whom he then felt
anger, sorrow, and pity.

> I wish they had been somewhere near me at that time,
> while I did not know that they were there, so that they
> could see my face and hear my voice as I read Psalm 4 at
> that time of rest, and perceive what that psalm wrought
> within me. . . . Would that they could have heard me,
> while I did not know that they heard me, so that they

22 Also: "Why then do I set out in order before you this account of so
many deeds? In truth, it is not that you may learn to know these matters from me, but that I may rouse up towards you my own affections,
and those of other men who read this, so that all of us may say: 'The
Lord is great and exceedingly to be praised' (Ps. 95:4)" (XI.1); "To
whom do I tell (*narro*) these things? Not to you, my God, but before
you (*apud te*) I tell them to my own kind, to mankind, or to whatever
small part of it may come upon these books of mine. Why do I tell
these things? It is that I myself and whoever else reads them may realize (*cogitemus*) from what great depths we must cry unto you"
(II.3). Confession is for God, narration is for human beings—even for
Augustine himself—so that they might think and confess. For the
sense of *cogito*, see X.11.

would not think that I said for their benefit the things that I uttered along with the words of the psalm. For in truth I would not say those same words, nor would I say them in the same way, if I knew that I was being heard and seen by them. Even if I said them, they would not understand them in the way that I spoke them in your presence, by myself and to myself out of the closest feelings of my mind. (IX.4)

Augustine's wish approximates the form of *Confessions*, but what the psalm wrought most deeply within him would be invisible to any human observer, and what Augustine said to God would be misunderstood by any Manichean.[23] Augustine overcomes these obstacles and expands the intended audience to all who can read or hear (X.3) by the actual form he gives *Confessions*.[24] Whereas he wished to have activated others' minds by making available a visible and audible, emotional display (in the belief that the most powerful rhetoric consists in the complete absence of rhetoric), his actual confessional voice represents those passionate moments as belonging to the past.[25] And whereas he wished to have others perceive (*per impossibile*) what God does within the soul, his written word publicizes as much as can appear of the inner life he has discovered. The rhetorical device of splitting himself into a present

23 Augustine had discovered that he himself was the source of his sins rather than, as the Manicheans believed, some other nature that sinned in him. "We are enlightened by you, so that we who were heretofore darkness may be light in you. Oh, if they would only see that inner eternal light, which I had tasted. I was sore grieved because I was not able to show it to them, even if they brought me their heart in those eyes of theirs that looked away from you, and if they said, 'Who will show us good things?'" (IX.4).

24 "Now, Lord, I confess to you in writing. Let him read it who wants to, let him interpret it as he wants" (IX.12).

25 See X.14. There Augustine distinguishes between passions and the memory of passions. "I am disturbed by none of these passions when I call them back to mind by remembrance of them."

confessional voice and a past restless heart enables him to speak more powerfully to whatever sort of reader finds him. The believer, the Manichean, the atheist, and all others may witness a drama that has already ended and judge the appropriateness of its denouement. At once sincere and ironic, he depends on charity to be believed (X.3), and his unguarded openness compels our trust.

Augustine displays his present confessional life by recollecting his discovery of Christian interior life as based in God the creator, but this interior life cannot appear in the world as it is in itself. The writing yields a visible copy of that life without being that life, and the copy activates us inwardly as it invites us to cultivate similar lives for ourselves. Ambrose's withdrawn and silent reading looked to Augustine like a retreat from the cares of the world, perhaps in order to return again to the world.[26] Augustine's writing is a return to the world from that inner life in order to call us away from absorption in the world and to our best life in intimate conversation with the creator.[27] As the Word of God reveals and calls us back to our previously hidden creator, so Augustine's *Confessions* reveals and calls us to an otherwise hidden life where we can dwell now with the creator. God is mediated necessarily by Christ,[28] and Augustine mediates that mediation.[29] God, who is before the world and beyond the world, is not distant, and Christ, who was sent but is no longer here among us, is not absent: God is "more inward than my inmost self, and superior to my highest being" (III.6).

---

26 See VI.3 and VI.11: "Ambrose has no leisure" (*non vacat Ambrosio*).

27 "Nor have you fashioned me to seek after those many other things, which are not what you are" (IX.4).

28 "I sought for a way of gaining strength sufficient for me to have joy in you, but I did not find it until I embraced 'the mediator between God and man, the man Christ Jesus, who is over all things, God blessed forever'" (VII.18; the internal quotation combines *1 Timothy* 2:5 with *Romans* 9:5). Cf. X.43.

29 Similarly, Ponticianus relates to Augustine the *story* of the conversion of others, and this precipitates Augustine's own conversion (VIII.6–7). And see XIII.21: "imitating the imitators of your Christ."

God's eternal Word lives in silence (XI.6) and yet speaks eternally and to us (XI.7–8). Above the sun and the moon and the stars are our own minds, which we transcend as we attain "the region of abundance . . . where life is that Wisdom by which all these things are made. . . . And this Wisdom itself is not made. . . . And while we discourse of this and pant after it, we attain to it in a slight degree by an effort of our whole heart" (IX.10). If only all created things would fall silent after saying they have not made themselves, then God's voice would be heard within (IX.10 and X.6). Augustine resists "the concupiscence of the flesh" (X.30) by his effort to regard food and other sources of pleasure as medicine (X.31). The desire for knowledge may degenerate into "concupiscence of the eyes," where even his desire to have some sign from God must be rejected as a sinful temptation: "In this vast forest, filled with snares and dangers, see how many of them I have cut away and thrust out of my heart" (X.35). "The ambition of the world," or the desire to be feared and loved by men "not because of you but in place of you" must give way to an austere attitude toward praise (X.37) in deference to God: "Let us be loved for your sake, and in us let only your Word be held in fear" (X.36). Augustine displays in writing the *conversatio* of a continent heart struggling (X.40) to love no earthly thing except in God:[30] "Let me not live my own life: badly

30 Even the love of human beings must be circumscribed. Augustine speaks of an excessive, pre-conversion grief over a dead friend: "Wretched was I, and wretched is every soul (*animus*) that is bound fast by friendship for mortal things" (IV.6). "But blessed is the man who loves you, and his friend in you. . . . For he alone loses no dear one to whom all are dear in him who is not lost. But who is this unless our God, the God who made heaven and earth . . . ?" (IV.9). The post-conversion reaction to the death of Nebridius is markedly different: "No longer does he put his ear to my mouth, but he puts his spiritual mouth to your fountain, and in accordance with his desire he drinks in wisdom, as much as he can, endlessly happy. Nor do I think that he is so inebriated by that fountain of wisdom as to become forgetful of me, for you O Lord, of whom he drinks, are mindful of us" (IX.3). His reaction to the death of Monica (IX.12) either belongs

have I lived from myself: I was death to myself: in you I live again. Speak to me, speak with me" (XII.10).[31] "This is the happy life, to rejoice over you, to you, and because of you: this it is, and there is no other" (X.22).

to a middle stage in which Augustine is wracked by extreme "human" sorrow he nonetheless hides successfully from others or it belongs to a deeper purification of his heart from earthly loves.

31 "But the living soul takes its beginning from the earth, for it profits no one except those faithful to keep continent from the love of this world, so that their soul may live to you, for it was dead while it lived in pleasures, in pleasures that bring death, O Lord" (XIII.21). In XIII.21, Augustine recapitulates the themes treated under the concupiscence of the flesh, the concupiscence of the eyes, and the ambition of the world (see X.30–38).

Assessing Augustine
Gavin Colvert

Introduction

*Do you realize what a debater's argument you are bringing up [Meno],
that a man cannot search either for what he knows or for what he does
not know? He cannot search for what he knows—since he knows it, there
is no need to search—nor for what he does not know, for he does not
know what to look for... I do not insist that my argument is right in all
other respects, but I would contend at all costs in both word and deed as
far as I could that we will be better men, braver and less idle, if we believe
that one must search for the things one does not [c] know, rather than if
we believe that it is not possible to find out what we do not know and
that we must not look for it.* (Plato Meno 80e–86b)[1]

Reading Plato in light of the challenges facing the contemporary
academy, we cannot help but observe that the more things change
in academia, the more they remain the same. Saint Augustine surely
had a similar thought as a result of his experience with the schools
of his day, and his encounter with Greek and Roman Platonism.
The examples of Plato and Augustine should teach us that many
of the core issues in liberal education are perennial. This is one reason why great works of literature, philosophy, and theology speak
meaningfully to us across the reaches of time, providing a sound
basis for liberal studies. Augustine's *Confessions* is just such a
book, and it has wisdom to offer the contemporary academy about
teaching and learning in spite of its ancient provenance. We can

1   Plato, John M. Cooper and G.M.A. Grube, trans., Five Dialogues
     (Hackett Publishing Co: 2010), pp. 70, 78.

begin to see this even from a cursory examination of the work's structure. Form serves function in the narrative. The intimate and recollective style of Augustine's writing is meant to effect a reorientation of the reader's thinking, rather than merely to transfer information or impart theoretical sophistication. Augustine's purpose is grounded in his understanding of how learning is possible and the limits of what it means to teach. Put succinctly, for Augustine all education is self-discovery. While his original audience may have found this style novel and even shocking, contemporary readers, who are accustomed to social media and reality television, will not find his use of first-person narrative strange. But they may find jarring his sustained conversation with God, mixed with Biblical, theological, philosophical and scientific reflection, because contemporary culture privatizes moral and religious convictions.

The source of the uneasiness we experience with the work may have changed, but our shared discomfort is a sign of a deeper perennial challenge, one which Augustine most definitely intends to provoke in the reader. He wanted to shake up the late Imperial Roman system of education in which he had participated both as a teacher and student, because it set aside substantive philosophical questions for an emphasis upon the forms of human eloquence and academic accomplishment. As a young man he was encouraged to read Cicero because of the master's eloquence, not because Cicero exhorted him in the *Hortensius* to live his life in a certain way.[2] In our own time, questions of form over substance again tend to dominate the academy. We attend to the forms of the curriculum and to the acquisition of certain generic skill-sets, such as reading, writing, quantifying, and analyzing, without being able to assess our progress with regard to deeper questions about truth and meaning. Some will argue that these more intangible goals are un-assessable

---

2   Saint Augustine, *Confessions* 3.4.7, in Rotelle, John E.; Maria Boulding, trans., *The Confessions* (New City Press: 1997) 79. All subsequent citations of the *Confessions* will be included parenthetically in the text in two ways: C will refer to the divisions in the *Confessions*, B to the pagination of Maria Boulding's translation.

in the narrow sense of the term, because they pertain to intellectual achievement and personal transformation, which are effected gradually over an entire life-time. Augustine would not reject that assertion. Yet the *Confessions* teaches us that attending to form over substance is a way of avoiding the more important things, because we despair of making progress with regard to them. In Augustine's day, skepticism was the fashionable philosophy at the root of this problem. Not that much has changed in the intervening sixteen hundred years. We Postmoderns speak a different and more radical, but analogous, skeptical idiom that is in some ways still continuous with Descartes' methodic doubt, which erected a high wall of separation between mind and world. Critics of Descartes have been successful in deconstructing his efforts to bridge the gap, but far less successful in their own efforts at breaching the wall. Contemporary perspectivism teaches us that all concepts are theory-laden and that we are trapped in our particular conceptual schemes.

What effect does this skepticism have upon contemporary education and culture? In his seminal work, *After Virtue*, Alasdair MacIntyre proposes the bold claim that the language and practice of morality have become fragmented. In the course of his argument, he discusses a revealing transformation of the way that we encounter religious literature and art:

> when we listen to the scripture because of what Bach wrote rather than because of what St. Matthew wrote, then sacred texts are being preserved in a form in which the traditional links with belief have been broken, even in some measure for those who still count themselves believers...a traditional distinction between the religious and the aesthetic has been blurred...[3]

MacIntyre's point about the transformation of religious and moral concepts into aesthetic categories provides a modern analogue of

3   Alasdair MacIntyre, After Virtue: A Study in Moral Theory (Indianapolis: University of Notre Dame Press, 1984) 38.

the educational experience of the young Augustine. The *Confessions* was composed in its peculiar introspective manner in order to break through the sort of encounter Augustine's classmates had with Cicero's *Hortensius* in school. The late antique academy treated it as an exercise in beautiful speech, without encouraging the reader or listener to appreciate the inherent beauty and power of Cicero's philosophical argument. Surface form dominated substance because fashionable intellectual currents in the academy, and broader cultural pressures, could no longer permit contemplation of the wisdom the text was proposing.

In no small measure because Augustine experienced an educational system in which the activity of the learner was disconnected from the wisdom of the texts studied, his theory of learning and his pedagogy stress that understanding is a personal achievement. It is entirely possible to be instructed about a text without profiting from its substance. Education is therefore not merely instruction or information transference, but a process of self-discovery. What appears to be a work all about Augustine himself, really concerns the transformation of the reader.[4] Augustine provides a form of recollection that we are invited to imitate, since it is only through self-reflection and self-assessment that understanding about the most important human questions is attainable. The very structure and style of the *Confessions* thus encourage the reader to resist ancient and contemporary tendencies to bracket questions that form the core of a genuine liberal education in order to concentrate upon more so-called "pragmatic" concerns.

It is a vitally contemporary work, because it forces the reader to reconsider the presuppositions and prejudices of our age. Augustine also provides a model for assessing and critiquing our

---

4 Thomas F. Martin, O.S.A. makes this point eloquently in his discussion of Augustine's *Confessions* as an example of Pieree Hadot's claim that ancient philosophy was a form of spiritual exercise. See: "Augustine's *Confessions* as Pedagogy: Exercises in Transformation," in Paffenroth, K., and K. L. Hughes, eds., *Augustine and Liberal Education*. Lexington Books, 2000, pp. 25–51.

educational enterprise. Indeed, for Augustine, we do not merely assess learning. Rather, learning is effected through a process of recollection and self-assessment. In this way, the *Confessions* provides both material for assessment in the form of an account that specifies the goals of a liberal education, and also a process or instrument by which that education is assessed and brought about. Concretely, were Augustine to be brought in as a consultant to today's academy, I believe that he would recommend we adopt a review process in which students and faculty engage in their own exercise of self-examination and recollection or "confessions."

A First Obstacle

Prior to embracing the thesis that Augustine can represent a paradigm for contemporary higher education, one must give careful consideration to several important types of objections. There are those who would assess Augustine as being a poor model for contemporary educators. In the first instance, on a practical level, critics may charge that his moral vision is simply too pious or too prudish to be of value. Without a doubt, his view of human excellence is distant from the cultural norms found on contemporary college campuses. In the second book of the *Confessions*, for example, he laments his preoccupation with sex at the age of sixteen and muses that "Some bounds might have been set to my pleasures if only the stormy surge of my adolescence had flung me up onto the shore of matrimony. Or again, if I had been... content to use my sexuality to procreate children as your law enjoins..." (C 2.3.3–4, B 63). Augustine goes even further, faulting himself for not having considered the higher calling of celibacy. These prescriptions may seem impossibly out of touch with our present reality. In response to this concern, it should be noted that Augustine is very well aware that his mature views in the *Confessions* are distant from the typical patterns of his own youth. Furthermore, while one can quarrel with what the mature Augustine thinks human beings can and ought to achieve, his insight into what causes young people to struggle in Book III is remarkably fresh, and even perhaps shock-ingly contemporary:

> Loving and being loved were sweet to me, the more so if I could also enjoy a lover's body...my boundless vanity made me long to appear elegant and sophisticated. I blundered headlong into the love which I hoped would hold me captive... I was loved, and I secretly entered into an enjoyable liaison, but I was also trammeling myself with fetters of distress, laying myself open to the iron rods and burning scourges of jealousy and suspicion, of fear, anger and quarrels.(C 3.1.1, B 75)

He even discusses a personal case of such a "liaison" taking place in a church in 3.3.5. Augustine would not have been terribly sur-prised by the "hooking up" culture on college campuses or by the emotional and personal suffering it can bring about. Moreover, given what he says about the voyeuristic aspects of his fascination with theatrical shows as a college student in Confessions 3.2.2, he would probably not have been surprised by the escalation of phe-nomena such as internet pornography. .

More significantly, if we think Augustine is only preoccupied with moral concerns about human sexuality and inebriation in Books II and III, we have missed the central moral point of those books entirely. In spite of the gravity with which he considers these issues, his abiding concern is to acknowledge that such things are often means of distracting oneself from the more challenging moral and intellectual struggle that faces young people. How else can one make sense of the supreme importance he places upon the episode of stealing some pears in Book II? This apparently inconsequential event worries him more greatly than all of the other prior bad choices he enumerates, and it is precisely the episode's apparent in-significance that is the source of his concern. He had been able to explain his other actions, at least in part, by appealing to the fog of adolescent desires and his parents' misplaced pride. But how se-riously should we take his satisfaction with these explanations, given what he learns about himself in light of the episode of with the pears? Taking the pears could not be attributed to some human need for food, or sex, or some other pleasure. Indeed, there was nothing about the pears themselves that made the theft attractive or irresistible.

Augustine comes face to face with his own freedom and his capacity for making bad choices. Freedom provides an explanation for his choice, but this explanation accentuates rather than diminishes his personal culpability: "Was I, in truth a prisoner, trying to simulate a crippled sort of freedom, attempting a shady parody of omnipotence by getting away with something forbidden? ...To do what was wrong simply because it was wrong—could I have found pleasure in that?"(C 2.6.14, B 71) Not surprisingly, there is a parallelism for Augustine between moral and intellectual maturity. Both require self-examination, self-mastery, self-understanding, and self-transformation, aided of course by divine grace. In addition, as with other ancient conceptions of the philosophical life, moral and theoretical excellence are intertwined. The virtues are and must continue to be understood as connected in structuring a liberal education.

Further Obstacles: Learning (and Teaching)

On the theoretical plane, there are at least two additional fundamental objections that must be considered: 1) that Augustine is actually an opponent of liberal education, which he sees as being opposed to Christian wisdom, and 2) that he thinks teaching and learning are impossible. Let us take the more extreme of these two theoretical objections first, although both of them are addressed in the *Confessions*. Responding to these objections will in turn provide a more comprehensive account of Augustine's vision of the nature and purposes of a liberal education.

There is a remarkable passage in Book I (8, 13) where Augustine describes the process of learning to speak as a young child. He initially admits that he has no recollection of this stage of his intellectual development, but he argues that, "You allow a person to infer by observing others what his own beginnings were like..." (C 1.6.10, B 44). This claim provides an important interpretive key for the *Confessions*. The introspective self-examination that constitutes the first nine books may appear on the surface to be a self-indulgent memoir, but it is rather a mirror in which the reader (or hearer) of the work can engage in his or her own process of self-examination and recollection. Thus, the literary form of the *Confessions* is a concrete expression of Augustine's pedagogy. This concrete expression is necessary because of his two key theses about teaching and learning: that all learning is self-discovery, not information transference, and second that Christ is the inner teacher (Augustine's quasi-Platonic theory of divine illumination):

> ...later I turned my attention to the way in which I had learned to speak. It was not that older people taught me by offering me words by way of formal instruction, as was the case soon afterward with reading. No, I taught myself, using the mind you gave me, O my God, because I was unable to express the thoughts of my heart by cries and inarticulate sounds and gestures in such a way as to gain what I wanted or make my entire meaning clear to everyone as I wished; so I grasped at words with my memory; when people called an object by some name, and while saying the word pointed to that thing. (C 1.8.13, B 47).

As M.F. Burnyeat has pointed out in his study of this passage, Ludwig Wittgenstein found Augustine's remarks suggestive and yet wrongheaded as a theory of language acquisition.[5] For Wittgenstein the principal difficulty with Augustine's model is that it proposes a 'Cartesian' view of mind and language, which holds that there is an inner mental language we possess, and the trick is to figure out

5   M. F. Burnyeat, "Wittgenstein and Augustine's *De magistro*," in *The Augustinian Tradition*, ed. Gareth Matthews, (Berkeley: University of California) p. 286.

how to map that language onto the words we hear and objects we see in the world. For Wittgenstein, Cartesian skepticism and solipsism must be rejected because we learn language and concepts in use. Furthermore, meaning is holistic. Wittgenstein suggests that while Augustine can make sense of words like "table,", which signify objects, he cannot make sense of other sentential components like prepositions or connectives, which alter the meaning of sentences, but do not signify objects in the world.

Burnyeat astutely replies that Augustine anticipated Wittgenstein's objection in the *De magistro,* his dialogue about teaching and learning. In that dialogue Augustine acknowledges that the way in which components of a sentence other than nouns signify is different from that of names, which signify objects in the world, and that such signification alters the meaning of a sentence. Hence the picture of language acquisition Wittgenstein elicits from Augustine's passage is too simplistic. Teaching does not take place merely by showing us signs for objects; rather, learning requires a holistic understanding of the meaning of signs. Thus, understanding is not the sort of thing that can be transmitted from teacher to learner as information.

This apparently minor point in the philosophy of language has significant implications for our more general understanding of Augustine's view of education. In the passage from the *Confessions* Augustine notes that it was not by instruction in signs from his elders that he learned to speak, but by the use of his own mind, given to him by God: he *taught himself* to speak. There is thus for Augustine a much more general problem, namely that no human being can teach another human being anything at all, if by teaching we mean the transference of information from one person to another.

In the *De magistro* Augustine reflects upon the activities of teaching and learning, showing us why "education" is very different from "instruction" as the root etymological meanings of those terms make clear. Liberal education aims to draw something out of the student, whereas the "instructor" imagines him or herself to be putting something into the student, some information for example, that was not already there. Augustine's discussion of language learning reminds teachers that it is not up to us to form the minds of our students, since properly speaking no human being can form another's mind or her understanding:

> Do teachers hold that it is their thoughts that are perceived and grasped rather than the very disciplines they take themselves to pass on by speaking? After all, who is so foolishly curious as to send his son to school to learn what the teacher thinks? When the teachers have explained by means of words all the disciplines they profess to teach, even the disciplines of virtue and of wisdom, then those who are called 'students' consider within themselves whether truths have been stated. They do so by looking upon the inner Truth, according to their abilities. That is therefore the point at which they learn. When they inwardly discover that truths have been stated, they offer their praises—not knowing that they are praising them not as teachers but as persons who have been taught, if their teachers also know what they are saying.[6]

Students become properly formed through education when they appropriate the truths they have learned for themselves, with the help of Christ, the "inner teacher." Simply put, formation is not information, and the "transformation of minds and hearts" contemplated by the *Confessions* is not something that teachers accomplish solely or even principally by their own efforts. Education is accomplished principally by the activity of the student.

Although Augustine's vision is distinctively theological, what he claims about teaching and learning is a perfectly general thesis, applicable equally to theology and biology. The claim that 'divine illumination' occurs does not entail that there is a specifically theological, or even mysterious, form or source of knowing in

6 Augustine and P. King (trans.), *Against the academicians; The teacher.* (Indianapolis: Hackett Publishing, 1995) p. 145.

disciplines such as mathematics or physics. Burnyeat suggests that this sort of thinking arises from a misperception of what is meant by 'divine illumination':

> The De magistro was Augustine's first extended presentation of his famous doctrine of internal illumination. The doctrine has been described as a misguided transference of of the idea of empirical vision into the intellectual sphere... Both [Plato and Augustine] are represented as holding that knowledge or understanding is an immediate relation to an isolated abstract object, in much the same way as seeing a table is a relation to a single physical object. Both philosophers are in fact saying the very opposite, that knowledge or understanding is of the connections between things, of things only as parts of a whole interrelated system; that is why, like empirical vision, it involves seeing things for oneself... All Augustine adds is that this Truth and this Light is God as present to our mind.[7]

According to Burnyeat, critics of Augustine's epistemology have exaggerated or misrepresented what he meant by internal illumination, treating it as cognitive access to an internal abstract object, such as a Platonic form, or direct acce1ss to the divine mind. But this interpretation [?] would simply add to the problem that Augustine is trying to solve both in the *Confessions* and the *De magistro*. Providing the mind with special access to some other abstract object does not solve the problem of how it is that we come to understand the signs that are used by others to represent and transmit their ideas. Illumination is not meant to be some supernatural or transcendent *third thing*, standing between mind and world, it is rather meant to be an observation about the mind's unique capacity to order things, appreciate their connections, and place them into a coherent account of the whole.

7   Burnyeat, p. 299.

This synthetic element in Augustine's account of learning to speak a language entails a non-linear component of how advances in our understanding within any domain take place. Our contemporary higher education assessment culture depends upon a set of premises about learning that are well-tailored to an understanding of teaching as information-transference. On that model, we can break down disciplinary goals and objectives into certain quantifiable or quasi-quantifiable skill-sets and bodies of information. Furthermore, progress in the field is roughly linear. Educational inputs should correlate with proximate educational outputs as measured by instruments that break progress down into measurable linear categories and are near to the immediate educational process.

We recognize, of course, that inputs do not always correspond to outputs in education. Good teaching does not always necessitate productive learning. But, for the most part, we presume that good inputs *typically* or *usually* lead to good outputs on the whole over time. Augustine's theory of learning cannot be reduced to a quibble about whether the linear model of teaching and learning is necessarily true or merely correct *ut in pluribus*. His concern is deeper than that. Given that learning is not a process of information-transfer, but instead depends upon personal understanding and integration, we should expect that inputs and outputs in the educational process are often not proximately connected to each other. While there may be some surface outcomes that fit the information-transfer model, the deepest and most important elements of a liberal education are certainly not this way. Learning is not fundamentally a process of sequentially constructing a database of knowledge and a set of skills, each of which can be mastered in abstraction from the other, any more than understanding the meaning of a sentence is merely a linear process of conquering the meanings of each of its components seriatim. Like Augustine's teachers, we will fail to understand the substance of a liberal education if we think about our pedagogical goals and purposes as concerned exclusively with equipping our students to excel in a speaking, calculating, analyzing, and debating contest.

Illuminating Learning: *Confessions* XI

One may be tempted to respond to the foregoing considerations by insisting that they infer too much from a single passage in Book I of the *Confessions*. The most appropriate Augustinian response to this concern is that one infers such conclusions from a comprehensive understanding of the work as a whole. This understanding ultimately cannot be separated from Augustine's life story, his purpose for telling it, his literary methods, his theological and philosophical premises, and many other such things. But to give some plausible support to the previous argument, let us consider briefly another passage, from *Confessions* XI, which is devoted to the nature of time and eternity. In Book XI Augustine offers the striking claim that time is none other than a 'dis-tension' in our consciousness, held together by memory. In the course of illustrating that point he discusses a line from St. Ambrose's hymn for the Liturgy of the Hours, *Deus creator omnium*:

> Obviously we measure any interval of time from some inception to some ending... Take the line, "Deus, creator omnium." This line consists of eight syllables, short and long alternating... Where is the short syllable I was going to use as a standard? What has become of the long one I want to measure? Both have made their sound, and flown away, and passed by, and exist no more... Evidently, then, what I am measuring is not the syllables themselves, which no longer exist, but something in my memory, something fixed and permanent there...In you, my mind, I measure time. Do not interrupt me by clamoring that time has objective existence... What I measure is the impression which passing phenomena leave in you, which abides after they have passed by: that is what I measure as a present reality, not the things that passed by so that the impression could be formed (C 11.27.34–36, B 307–8).

Augustine's point about time, which is like our grasp of a line of music or poetry, is that it is only something meaningful because the whole thing is grasped together in memory. Time exists in the mind alone. He is no solipsist when he says this. Rather, his point is that like the meaning of a sentence, a length of time can only be grasped as something whole when it is held together in the understanding by memory.

In the same way, a liberal education is not something that happens seriatim—a few syllables here and there—it is only something if and when it becomes a coherent expanse of growth in understanding and wisdom in the mind of the student. Concentrating one's efforts upon the syllables while losing sight of the lyrics was a genuine problem in Augustine's day, and it threatens to be a continual problem in our own time.

Is teaching impossible, though, and has Augustine given in to Meno's paradox of inquiry that we cannot learn what we do not know? The short answer to this question is "no," although it would be "yes" if we conceive of teaching strictly as information transfer. There is much more that ought to be said about Augustine's view of teaching in the *Confessions*. Doing so would require a comprehensive appreciation of his conception of the relationship between philosophical wisdom and religious faith, as well as his doctrine of Christ as the "inner teacher." Augustine's epistemology, theology, and pedagogy are therefore inseparable. At this point we must content ourselves with a glimpse of this nexus from the opening lines of *Confessions* I, which introduce a theological conundrum with broader epistemological and pedagogical significance. Augustine writes:

> Grant me to know and understand, Lord, which comes first: to call upon you or to praise you? To know you or to call upon you? Must we know you before we can call upon you? Anyone who invokes what is still unknown may be making a mistake. Or should you be invoked first, so that we may then come to know you? But how can people call upon someone in whom they do not yet believe? (C 1.1.1, B 39)

The attentive reader will notice at least two points from the previous discussion: first, that Augustine is offering a theological version of the paradox of inquiry, and second, that he is contrasting knowing or understanding and believing. This contrast is familiar to us from Plato, who makes a distinction between true belief and knowledge. Just as Plato's Socrates in the *Meno* wants to find a pathway from ignorance to scientific knowledge that leads through right opinion, Augustine's epistemology requires a clear understanding of the place of right opinion or belief in general (and also religious faith in particular), as a foundation for understanding. Thus, while no human being can form another human being's mind so as to produce understanding, there is an important place for belief in teaching, and also for critical appreciation of how to evaluate the credibility of belief on the part of the learner. So, for example, there are a great many true beliefs one must acquire about evolutionary theory or quantum physics in order to be initiated into the study of those fields, before one can undertake critical inquiry. Those kinds of things are appropriately communicated to the learner in the classroom. One must inhabit a field of study for a while (we might say colloquially, "take it on faith") before he or she grasp it, but there is a non-linear stage of development at which the learner begins to appropriate and understand the field of study. If we fail to appreciate the distinct but important relationship between those states, we may fall into serious pedagogical errors. A full and careful study of the account of teaching and learning in the *Confessions* will therefore vindicate the conclusion that Augustine does not reject the importance of teaching in spite of his qualification that teaching is not merely information transfer.

Against Liberal Education?

As surprising as it may seem, there are those who think that Augustine's *Confessions* provides a poor paradigm for reflecting upon the value and purpose of liberal education because he was actually an opponent of this kind of human endeavor. Understanding this line of argument requires some grasp of the intellectual transformation effected by his conversion to Christianity. As we learn in third and fourth books of the *Confessions,* he was classically educated as a rhetorician from a very young age—essentially he went to and later taught at a law school. His parents spared no expense, probably going beyond prudential use of their assets, in order to provide him the finest education possible, so that he could have a successful career. By all accounts, Augustine was a remarkably talented student and a successful orator. He subsequently held teaching posts in Carthage, Rome, and Milan. The ancient equivalent of student loans posed a problem for him, and the students were not always attentive to their studies, but otherwise he had a very successful rise in prominence. His mother, Monica, carefully arranged a marriage to insure the success of his career and followed him from teaching post to teaching post, as he climbed the academic ladder of late imperial Rome. Because of his classical education and his reading of philosophical works, especially the neo-Platonists, Augustine came to see the cult of Manicheanism as intellectually suspect, and after leaving it behind as a dalliance of his youth, he converted to Christianity. His tremendous rhetorical skill and classically trained mind evidently contributed to his ability to be an effective preacher, and ultimately, the author of the *Confessions* itself. He would therefore appear to be a good example of the value of a classical curriculum.

After his conversion, however, Augustine had harsh things to say about his college experience, about the shallow minds of his teachers, and about his own teaching career, which he likened to a form of prostitution in the *Confessions* and other works such as *De doctrina christiana.* Traditionally, many have regarded the *Confessions* and *De doctrina* as proposing a reform of liberal education, which is complementary to the work of his earlier philosophical dialogues. But recently, others have suggested that Augustine wished to reject the whole enterprise. Kevin Hughes, for example, argues that it is "ironic" to think of Augustine as a proponent of liberal education:

> Prior to his conversion, Augustine was an academic, and, one might say, one of the young budding "public

intellectuals" of late Roman imperial culture. And yet it seems his conversion was precisely a conversion away from the world of the academy... Christian conversion is for Augustine an exodus from bondage, and to "despoil the Egyptians" was to "cram" oneself with...the wealth of pagan culture as one...abandoned that culture... Should we speak rather of Augustine or Liberal Education?[8]

Hughes' reference to "despoiling the Egyptians" recalls one of the metaphors Augustine uses in the *De doctrina christiana* to explain why and how Christian interpreters of Biblical texts ought to appropriate insights from secular wisdom into their study. For Augustine, every form of human wisdom, regardless of its proximate source, comes ultimately from the divine source. Thus, there is nothing illicit in making use of sources of knowledge in history, science, psychology, logic, rhetoric, etc., in order to grasp more effectively the Biblical text. Hughes' point is that despite Augustine's willingness to take over these sources, the secular enterprise is regarded as suspect, and the appropriation of secular wisdom ends up being somewhat piecemeal in being adapted to the foreign purpose of Biblical exegesis out of its original context. Thus, while some of the tools of liberal education are preserved, Hughes contends that the academy as an enterprise and its curriculum are rejected by the mature Augustine.

One must remember, of course, the context of *De doctrina christiana*. Augustine does not argue that Biblical exegesis is the only legitimate form of human inquiry, nor that our appropriation of pagan wisdom must always be piecemeal and adapted to a foreign theological purpose. ButHughes makes his case against treating Augustine as a critical friend of liberal education stronger by pointing to the parallelism of his rejection of his academic career and his repudiation of his former carnal and sexual vices:

8   Kevin Hughes, "The 'Arts Reputed Liberal': Augustine on the Perils of Liberal Education," in K. Paffenroth and K.L. Hughes, *Augustine and Liberal Education* (Lexington Books, 2008) p. 95.

Augustine's portrait of his life as a teacher suggests that he sees academia only as a subtle variation on such carnal temptations. From this perspective, the *Confessions* is as much the tale of Augustine's turning away from his liberal education as from his carnal habits... Augustine and his friends are nothing better than high class prostitutes that enjoy their work a bit too much. They are, he says, both seducer and seduced, both deceivers and deceived. The public face of their deceptions, says Augustine, is through their engagement with the "arts reputed liberal." His teaching is a practice of mutual seduction and manipulation, of "selling talkative skills apt to sway others."[9]

Looking at the beginning of *Confessions* IV, to which Hughes refers, there is a certain degree of plausibility to this argument. Augustine describes the period of his education and subsequent career in academia in terms of seduction (*seducebamur et seducebamus*) and certain desires (*cupiditatibus*), that imply a direct comparison with carnal desire:

> Throughout those nine years, from my nineteenth to my twenty-eighth year, I and others like me were seduced and seducers, deceived ourselves and deceivers of others amid a welter of desires: publicly through the arts reputed "liberal," and secretly under the false name of religion... During these years I was teaching the art of rhetoric, selling talkative skills apt to sway others because greed swayed me. (C 4.2.2, B 93)

There is an underlying presupposition here, however, that must be contested. Augustine regarded his adolescent sexual exploits as sinful, and he eventually chose a life of celibacy, making himself "a eunuch for the kingdom of God" (C 2.2.3 and 8.1.2). But, he

9   Hughes, p. 96.

did not regard either marriage or human sexuality as bad in themselves, and he did not intend to claim that all human beings ought to refrain from them as evil. He did hold that carnal desire, which had become insubordinate to the will, was evil and that in our present state it was essentially inseparable from married life, which was still good in spite of this. It should be noted that this is a different matter from that of whether he regarded the celibate life as superior in a way. Whether he succeeds in making his case, Augustine vigorously contests the view of Jovinian that one must be a Manichean and despise bodily intercourse as evil if he holds the superiority of holy virginity.[10] It is one thing to endorse celibacy as a greater sacrifice for the good of the Church and even as a purification of one's own weaknesses. It is quite another thing to regard human sexual interaction as fundamentally evil. That would be to treat Augustine as a Manichean. Of course, he was a Manichean at one time, but it was precisely the dualistic treatment of matter as evil and spirit as good that Augustine repudiated when he argued that everything is good, insofar as it has being, and evil is a privation or distortion of something good. The claim that evil is *not* something—*not* a substance, is *not* the claim that evil is not real. It is very real, but it is a twisted form of goodness, since everything good comes from the absolutely original source of our being. To treat sexuality as fundamentally perverse is inconsistent with Augustine's broader theological program on many levels. We ought not to dismiss him as a prude because of his honest assessment of the over-sexualized atmosphere of his college experience. We may differ with his assessment of the nature and purpose of conjugal love, but we should not mistake that for Manichean dualism. Doing so inclines us to miss what Augustine regards as the far deeper and more dangerous personal failings of pride, the perverse exercise of his freedom, and the unwillingness to acknowledge the source of his being.

10 See e.g., *De Nuptiis et Concupiscentia* Bk. II.38 (23) in Nicean and Post-Nicean Fathers, Series I Vol. 5, (Grand Rapids: Eerdmans, [2005]), p. 857.

In the same way, Augustine regards as dangerous the seductiveness of academic life and Manichean religion. Curiously, he thinks that his joining of the Manichean cult was more dangerous than literary studies because, unlike the lessons of his college professors, he took Manicheanism seriously as claiming something true about the world.[11] But, just as human sexuality is not intrinsically evil, when its role and purposes are properly appreciated, and the source of its goodness is acknowledged, so the enterprise of liberal education need not be regarded as intrinsically evil, even though Augustine himself chose to set aside his academic career. In his case there were other good reasons for doing so, and he also knew that, like his sexual desires, he found the allure of academic life intoxicating, in such a way that he was distracted by the pursuit of personal acclaim over human excellence. Perhaps most significantly, Augustine's concern about academic life was that, as practiced in the ancient world (and, we might argue, as it is practiced today) it placed form over substance, eloquence over truth. In some cases, such as Augustine's attraction to his teachers because of their reputations and public acclaim, it even placed a kind of false indoctrination over the quest for wisdom. When the teacher becomes a guru, teaching ceases to be assisting in the quest for self-understanding, and it becomes a cult of personality, neglecting the true source of wisdom. All of these are serious vices to which academics and their pupils are liable. Augustine understood their danger, but we must avoid leaping to the conclusion that he wished to condemn human sexuality or education as such:

> Furthermore, what profit was it to me that I, rascally
> slave of selfish ambitions that I was, read and understood

11 See C 3.6.11, B 82, "The fables of schoolmasters and poets are far better than the snares then being set for me; yes, verses, songs and tales of Medea in flight are undeniably more wholesome than myths about the five elements being metamorphosed to defeat the five caverns of darkness. These latter have no truth in them at all and are lethal to anyone who believes them."

by myself as many books as I could get concerning the so-called liberal arts? I enjoyed these, not recognizing the source of whatever elements of truth and certainty they contained. I had turned my back to the light and my face to the things it illuminated, and so no light played upon my own face, or on the eyes that perceived them. Whatever I understood of the arts of grammar and rhetoric, of dialectic, geometry, music and arithmetic, without much difficulty or tuition from anyone, I understood because my swift intelligence and keen wits were your gift. (C 4.16.30, B 110)

The previous passage suggests that liberal education itself is not bad, but that it can become distorted when we lose sight of it source and purposes, especially when that distortion is effected by the very educational program itself.

Looking more closely at *Confessions* III, we can see that this was Augustine's own educational experience. In his case, these difficulties were fueled both by internal and external obstacles. Both of these sets of obstacles seem shockingly fresh and contemporary when we consider them. Externally, his teachers were focused upon superficial pedagogical objectives. Internally, Augustine's college experience was impacted by a restlessness for life that might easily be described as the consequence of a certain kind of boredom:

So I arrived at Carthage, where the din of scandalous love-affairs raged cauldron-like around me. I was not yet in love, but I was enamored with the idea of love, and so deep within me was my need that I hated myself for the sluggishness of my desires. In love with loving, I was casting about for something to love...the security of a way of life free from pitfalls seemed abhorrent to me, because I was inwardly starved of that food. (C 3.1.1, B 75)

Shortly, thereafter he immerses himself in frenzied efforts to experience, vicariously, sadness and joy:

Why is it that one likes being moved to grief at the sight of sad or tragic events on stage, when one would be unwilling to suffer the same things oneself? In the capacity of spectator one welcomes sad feelings; in fact, the sadness itself is the pleasure. What incredible stupidity! The more a person is buffeted by such passions in his own life, the more he is moved by watching similar scenes on stage, although his state of mind is usually called misery when he is undergoing them himself and mercy when he shows compassion for others so afflicted. But how real is the mercy evoked by fictional dramas? The listener is not moved to offer help, but merely invited to feel sorrow; and the more intensely he feels it the more highly he rates the actor in the play. (C 3.2.2, B 76)

What is going on here? Augustine arrives at Carthage, desperate to feel alive. His whole "high school" career has been a preparation for this moment of embarking upon real life and future success. Finally he arrives, with his eagerly supportive parents in the background, imagining future conquests on the professional stage. Unfortunately, it doesn't seem all that exciting, and his teachers are preoccupied with a set of apparently superficial objectives that have very little to do with what is really eating away at his *psyche*. He and his fellow classmates begin to ask themselves, "When does life really become interesting? Is this it?"

Augustine and his friends are moved by the desire for what we may call ethical and psychological tourism. They want to feel happy and also sad—vicariously of course—because they are looking for (*ersatz*) experiences that can deliver the sense of living large, of really being alive for the first time. Note how Augustine says that the security of a life free from difficulties is "abhorrent" to him. He literally wants to live on the edge—without really getting hurt. Sex, drugs, rock and roll, and the ancient equivalent of reality-TV provide the raw materials for that experience of living large. His liberal education does not provide it, in part because he and his classmates are unprepared to accept that it can. As we have already noted, they did not take the teaching seriously as addressing meaningful questions. But, in truth, the teaching wasn't addressing meaningful questions, because it was preoccupied with syllogisms, propositions, forms of eloquence, syllables, etc., to the exclusion of the deeper purposes of the texts they were studying. Perhaps these were attainable goals, or perhaps his teachers couldn't agree upon any answers to these deeper questions, so they avoided them entirely as beyond their purposes.

The surprising thing is that Augustine was remarkably "successful" as a student in spite of all this. Somehow he managed not to allow his "strolling through the streets of Babylon" (C 2.3.8) with his classmates by night to interfere with his studies by day.

> The prestigious course of studies I was following looked as its goal to the law-courts, in which I was destined to excel and where I would earn a reputation all the higher in the measure that my performance was the more unscrupulous. So blind can people be that they glory even in their blindness! Already I was the ablest student in the school of rhetoric. At this I was elated and vain and swollen with pride. (C 3.3.6, B 78).

The nature of Augustine's "success," however, is in question. The mature Augustine writing the *Confessions* knows there is something deeply wrong with the education in the "arts reputed liberal" that he was receiving. But the young Augustine understood this too, even if not explicitly. The academy taught him to expect a certain kind of success from his studies, and nothing more. Augustine diligently milked his academic work for every benefit he thought it could provide, and he was pleased when his teachers praised him for his efforts. In this sense, he blindly contented himself with what he was doing in school. But, at the same time, he was drawn in by Manichean dualism. The Manichees were deeply attractive to Augustine because they professed to have the answers to the questions that were really tearing at his soul. The mature Augustine who writes the *Confessions* recognizes this was a very impoverished path to pursue, but the young Augustine fell under the influence of a cult, suspending even the critical and analytical abilities he was mastering in school, because of the urgency of the desire to find answers and to know what his purpose was—to understand how to be really alive. Manicheanism and "Survivor" served the same need, even if they did so in very different ways.

> I was being subtly maneuvered into accepting the views of those stupid deceivers by the questions they constantly asked me about the origin of evil, and whether God was confined to a material form with hair and nails, and whether people who practiced polygamy, killed human beings and offered animal sacrifices could be considered righteous. Being ignorant of these matters I was very disturbed by the questions, and supposed that I was approaching the truth when I was in fact moving away from it. I did not know that evil is nothing but the diminishment of good to the point where nothing at all is left. (C 3.7.12, B 83)

In the middle of all this seeking after "success" in his career path, and vicariously attempting to live large, there was one academic experience that was very different. Oddly enough, it was occasioned by a teacher, although that was not the professor's purpose. As a classroom exercise, Augustine picks up Cicero's *Hortensius*:

> In the customary course of study I had discovered a book by an author called Cicero, whose language is almost universally admired, though not its inner spring. This book of his is called the *Hortensius* and contains an exhortation to philosophy. The book changed my way of feeling and the character of my prayers to you, O Lord, for under its influence my petitions and desires altered. All my hollow hopes suddenly seemed worthless, and with unbelievable intensity my heart burned with longing for the immortality that wisdom seemed to promise...

My interest in the book was not aroused by its usefulness in the honing of my verbal skills...for it had won me over not by its style but by what it had to say. (C 3.4.7, B 79).

What should we make of this narrative of Augustine's encounter with Ciceronian philosophy? If we are able to grant that his experience of being a student and eventually a young professional is substantially similar to that of contemporary students in important ways—and I would maintain that is so—then assessing Augustine's experience may be very helpful to us in the contemporary academy, even if he turns out to be an opponent of liberal education. At the very least, there is a case to be made for a more careful selection of texts that we ought to be placing in student's hands, even when those texts are being studied for more practical purposes. Indeed, being more intentional about what we ask our students to read may be the single most important teaching decision we make, since as Augustine argues, learning is a non-linear process of growing in self-understanding, and we have no way of assessing precisely how and when students are going to have a transformative experience through what they are reading.

But there are other important lessons here. We should not take initial resistance on the part of students to the study of deeply human questions as a sign of their disinterest, but more as a sign of the confusing and uncertain stage of life in which they find themselves. Were Augustine to have received a more deeply thoughtful introduction to Cicero's philosophical ideas with the assistance of his teachers, he might have been better able as a young man to resist the false allure of Manicheanism. Furthermore, we should not underestimate the capacity of a classical work to have a significant effect upon students, nor should we doubt that they really do have deeply human questions that concern them. Apathy in the classroom is a strange manifestation of a kind of unwillingness to confront the very things that often most concern us.

Perhaps the most important conclusion we ought to take away from Augustine's experience of a liberal education is that we should never allow concern with superficial forms of academic achievement and the marketable skills we think it should provide to overtake the substance of deeper human concerns that cannot be more easily assessed, because progress in them is holistic, non-linear, and dependent upon the student. The academy lowers itself when it does this, but it also diminishes for the student the horizon of expectations for what an education should be. To most of us in academia, this will seem something like an obvious truth, one that we don't need to worry about, because *we* after all do not teach that way. Should we not be given pause, however, by the fact that this is a perennially recurring problem in the academy? It was true in Augustine's day. It was arguably the case with decadent forms of scholasticism at the end of the Middle Ages and prior to the Renaissance. This recurring phenomenon is not a mere coincidence. This, in turn, is where Augustine's dissatisfaction with "the arts reputed liberal" lies.

For him, the vices of pride, jealousy, greed, and selfishness are common features of academic life, because scholars are usually intellectually gifted people. Where there is great potential for good, there is also the greatest potential for corruption. Perhaps this is why Augustine compares the vices of the academy to those of carnal desire—not because he despises either the academy or the body (he has repudiated Manicheanism after all), but because the goodness of God's creation is more easily distorted the more something is in being. The capacity to create a likeness of ourselves, which identity is passed down through the generations, and the ability to have intimate communion with another human being are both images of divine perfection and creativity. They are among the highest achievements of human life, and as such they are also liable to distortion, misuse, and suffering. In the same way, the potential of a liberal education to facilitate growth in wisdom is remarkable, but the allure of academic vices such as intellectual pride and greed for honors, can be hard to resist. Put simply, liberal education cannot have the capacity for such destruction and suffering, unless there is some very great good at stake that can be distorted. This is the necessary implication of Augustine's embrace of the Christian response to the Manichean problem of evil.

Kevin Hughes, however, remains committed to the thesis that Augustine was an opponent rather than a critical friend of liberal education. Augustine's image of "despoiling the Egyptians" as a model for the appropriation of the liberal arts in scriptural study and interpretation in the *De doctrina christiana* remains central to his thinking in this way. As Hughes sees it, appropriating the spoils of Pagan culture means wresting them piecemeal from the discarded super-structure of the classical curriculum:

> It is important to note that even this image [despoiling the Egyptians] represents conversion as an exodus, a departure from the culture of liberal education and philosophy that had previously enslaved these great figures like Israel under Pharoah. Any treasures that are taken are piecemeal and cut loose from the web of the oppressive culture left behind. The insights of rhetoric and philosophy will no longer be part of a system or an institution of liberal education per se, but instead be applied ad hoc to the understanding of Scripture. (Hughes, 99)

We can acknowledge several elements of Hughes' argument that seem correct. First, it is certainly true that Augustine explicitly rejects the notion that the *De doctrina* can serve as a treatise on eloquence, or any other liberal art for that matter. Second, Augustine himself was eager to escape the prideful and seductive world of academia, never to return. Third, a Christian ordering of wisdom would require a fairly radical rethinking of certain elements of the curriculum he encountered in school, both as to its subject matter and the nature of the formation envisioned. But Hughes' interpretation of Augustine's criticism as a wholesale repudiation of the liberal arts (properly understood) is an exaggeration of Augustine's program. His departure from the world of trafficking in speechifying and his adaptation of elements of a liberal education for Biblical interpretation do not constitute a systematic indictment of systematicity. Such an indictment would entail a fairly low estimate of the project of Christian wisdom. In addition, Augustine's choice of life and the subject matter of his works do not exclude the possibility that others may choose different intellectual paths, so long as they resist falling into the vices that too often accompany academic pursuits.

His treatment of matters concerning liberal education in the *De doctrina christiana* helps to support the foregoing conclusion. In DDC 2.26, for example, he argues that there is nothing inherently wrong with the study of the liberal arts. They are useful for the study of the Bible, to be sure, but "usefulness" does not necessarily entail that systematic study of the liberal arts is fundamentally corrosive:

> Those [studies], on the other hand, which relate to the mutual intercourse of men, are, so far as they are not matters of luxury and superfluity, to be adopted, especially the forms of the letters which are necessary for reading, and the various languages as far as is required— a matter I have spoken of above... All these are useful, and there is nothing unlawful in learning them, nor do they involve us in superstition, or enervate us by luxury, if they only occupy our minds so far as not to stand in the way of more important objects to which they ought to be subservient. (DDC 2.26)

In his discussion of taking over liberal studies from Pagan culture ("plundering the Egyptians"), Augustine envisions the primary importance of teaching the Gospel, and the usefulness of liberal learning as a tool for that enterprise. But he also acknowledges that whole institutions of secular culture can have value, insofar as they are not contrary to human well-being.[12] In a passage (DDC 2.39)

---

12 See DDC 2.40: "For, as the Egyptians had not only the idols and heavy burdens which the people of Israel hated and fled from, but also vessels and ornaments of gold and silver...all branches of heathen learning have not only false and superstitious fancies...but they contain also liberal instruction which is better adapted to the use of the

SO ANCIENT SO NEW

that Hughes sees as a recommendation for young people to avoid liberal studies altogether, Augustine warns about the pursuit of the classical curriculum as a false means to the attainment of human happiness, but not as something inherently unworthy of study.[13] The worthiness of the classical liberal arts is consistent with Augustine's broader argument, found in works such as the *City of God,* that the Christian conception of the ultimate end of human life differs from that of pagan philosophy. Furthermore, in the very passage that Hughes takes as Augustine's definitive repudiation of the study of the liberal arts, Augustine recommends the study of rhetoric, which he asserts is not his purpose in the *De doctrina,* but which therefore must be studied systematically outside of his works:

> In the first place, then, I wish by this preamble to put a stop to the expectations of readers who may think that I am about to lay down rules of rhetoric such as I have learnt, and taught too, in the secular schools, and to warn them that they need not look for any such from me. Not that I think such rules of no use, but that whatever use they have is to be learnt elsewhere; and if any good man should happen to have leisure for learning them, he is not to ask me to teach them either in this work or any other...Now, the art of rhetoric being available for the enforcing either of truth or falsehood, who

truth...These, therefore, the Christian...ought to take away from them, and to devote to their proper use in preaching the gospel. Their garments, also,—that is, human institutions such as are adapted to that intercourse with men which is indispensable in this life,—we must take and turn to a Christian use."

13 See DDC 2.39: "I think that it is well to warn studious and able young men, who fear God and are seeking for happiness of life, not to venture heedlessly upon the pursuit of the branches of learning that are in vogue beyond the pale of the Church of Christ, as if these could secure for them the happiness they seek; but soberly and carefully to discriminate among them."

will dare to say that truth in the person of its defenders is to take its stand unarmed against falsehood? For example, that those who are trying to persuade men of what is false are to know how to introduce their subject, so as to put the hearer into a friendly, or attentive, or teachable frame of mind, while the defenders of the truth shall be ignorant of that art? Since, then, the faculty of eloquence is available for both sides, and is of very great service in the enforcing either of wrong or right, why do not good men study to engage it on the side of truth, when bad men use it to obtain the triumph of wicked and worthless causes, and to further injustice and error? (DDC 4.1–2)

It is difficult to understand how Augustine could have thought that young people should avoid liberal studies altogether, and that no one ought to specialize in the liberal arts, at the same time that he recommends the study of rhetoric. The best way to make sense of these various passages is to recognize that the problem lies not in the discipline itself, but in what we may wrongfully expect from it, and in the common tendency of academia to engender various intellectual vices. It is very difficult to accomplish, but if a liberal education helps us to properly order our loves, then perhaps there will be nothing in it that is contrary to Christian wisdom.

Conclusions

In order to conclude, let us return briefly to the memorable story of Augustine's theft of the pears in *Confessions* II. The episode takes place just prior to embarking upon his 'college' education. As such, it encapsulates much of what we have been considering with regard to his account of teaching, learning and liberal education. The mature Augustine is able to assess the moral quality of his actions at an earlier age, because of his growth in understanding through the recollective process which is his *Confessions*. The *Confessions* gives us an indication of what Augustine would have to say about how to assess the effectiveness of our educational aims, purposes and outcomes. The *book* itself, its style of writing, its introspective mode of reflection, and the act of recollection which it constitutes, is Augustine's model of assessment. His style reflects his pedagogy and his theory of teaching and learning. Learning is not simply information-transference, nor is it strictly linear in its development. Signs do not, of themselves, teach anything. Education takes place in the recollective act of the student who reflects upon what the teacher or the text has attempted to communicate. Because understanding requires the pre-disposition of the will to love things rightly, as well as the work of memory and intelligence holding things together and interpreting them, progress in understanding of the most important things is non-linear. There is no simple correlation between educational inputs and outputs.

The youthful Augustine tends to externalize his moral failings in terms of compulsion. His desires, "dragged me, young and weak as I was…and engulfed me in a whirlpool of sin." (2.2.2) The mature Augustine is able to see that there was "no motive for my malice except malice…I was in love with my own ruin." What Augustine realizes in reflecting upon this apparently senseless and insignificant act is the place of his own freedom in his choices, and his own responsibility for the self-destructive path leading away from God. Could this realization have taken place at sixteen, or even nineteen or twenty-eight years of age? It surely could, but its occurrence depended not upon Augustine's teachers, but upon himself. As the wise old Bishop advised his mother Monica, when she wanted him to disabuse Augustine of his Manicheanism, he was better left to his books than to external efforts at refutation. Augustine was prepared to listen to his books, but he was not prepared to listen to his mother. There is no magic in signs, whether they be spoken or written. Teachers can make their efforts to communicate, but learning can only be effected by students themselves. We can't solve the problems of the moral purposes of liberal education by a course in ethics, for example, any more than the Bishop could have turned Augustine around in his twenties by having an argument with him.

Because there are no easy solutions we are tempted either to dispose of such courses, or to evaluate their usefulness in terms of linear progress in some peripheral skill we can measure. But, if we do so, we become the post-modern equivalent of Augustine's teachers, and the cycle will continue. It would be better for us to place good food before our students and to labor over the answers to the most important questions, hoping that they will profit from these things, even as Augustine profited from reading the *Hortensius*. The best we can do is encourage that self-discovery at an earlier stage of development by occasioning the sort of introspective recollection about the deepest and most important human questions as Augustine does in his *Confessions*.

Rousseau's "Illumination" and Augustine's "Conversion": On Substantial Change
Leonard R. Sorenson

My intention in this essay is to address the question of the "influence" of Augustine on Rousseau through the lens of Augustine's account of his "Conversion" and Rousseau's account of his "Illumination." I argue to the conclusions that Augustine's "Conversion" did influence Rousseau; that Augustine constituted a challenge to Rousseau; that Rousseau's "Illumination" scene was intended to supersede the influence of Augustine on humanity; and that both authors constitute a challenge to us.[1]

---

1   Citations to Rousseau are to C. Kelly. *The Confessions and Correspondence, Including the Letter to Malesherbes.* The Collected Works of Rousseau. Vol. 5. Dartmouth College. The University Press of New England. 1995. This work is cited K. below. Also cited is V. Gourevitch. *Rousseau, The Discourses and Other Early Political Writings.* Cambridge University Press. 1997. This work is cited G. below. Citations to Augustine refer to M. Boulding. *The Confessions. Saint Augustine.* New City Press. Hyde Park. 1997. The work is cited B. below. Rousseau's "Illumination" scenes proper are in Book VIII of his *Confessions,* (K. 243–245,) and his *Second Letter to Malesherbes* (574–577) which, in turn, are substantially informed by his first extended autobiography, his sequel to the *First Discourse,* namely, his *Preface to Narcissus, or on the Lover of Himself.* Both the latter and the *Discourse on Inequality* begin and end on the theme of self-knowledge, though the former, as autobiography is wholly limited to that theme (G. 92–124; 92:106,124: 1 and its n.). Augustine's "Con-

Preliminary evidence strongly suggests that our question is indeed a very worthy question. Augustine's "Conversion" and Rousseau's "Illumination" scenes are found in the same part of their books both entitled *Confessions*. Both works are autobiographies which presuppose some kind and degree of self-knowledge. Both authors follow in their own ways the Delphic Oracle: "Know Thyself." Both authors agree that memory and judgment of the relevant memories are conditions of the possibility of self-knowledge. Both authors also presuppose a certain distance from others and the world. Both authors agree that we must be embodied awareness—awareness of our embodied soul, mind, self and other than our self, the world—and that our embodied self is formed and informed by our embodied soul, mind, others and the world. This distance—this double distance, embodied awareness of *awareness of*—is a condition of possibility of the quest for self-knowledge and therefore of autobiography.[2] Both authors also agree that the quest for self-knowledge requires a comprehensive exploration not only into our embodied soul and mind but also into the world and our place in the world. Both authors therefore take the Delphic Oracle to point to the all-important question of what is the right or best way of life, which entails the question of what we ought to love:

> version" scene proper is in Chapter VIII (B.150–157). In both cases I spare the Reader—and myself—voluminous notes. The originals cover a small number of pages that one simply must read for oneself. There are two fine secondary sources from which I benefited, even as I differ from them in important ways: A. Hardle, *The Modern Self in Rousseau's Confessions: A Reply to St, Augustine*. University of Notre Dame Press,1983; and P. Riley. *Character and Conversion in Autobiography*. University of Virginia Press, 2004.

2   124:1 and its note. This distance is understood and hence experienced by Christians as a consequence of the Fall. Christians are therefore Pilgrims lost in the cosmos. Existentialists, derivative from Heidegger, understand and hence experience the distance in a different way, as do those who are "alienated." B. IX: 150; VIII and X. Rousseau **seems** to approach this distance as an opportunity to search for what is truly good for him.

what is truly lovable. Both authors speak of transcendence, of supra-rational reality, of the heart that entails secrets that the head cannot fathom, and that therefore complete and certain self-knowledge is impossible.

What is more, both authors also agree that autobiography, in any meaningful sense, presupposes a sort of self-importance. Autobiography presupposes that one's way of life is somehow important enough for others to become aware of it, to take the time to read about it. Both authors agree that autobiography constitutes a challenge, by way of comparison by the reader, to the way of life of the reader. Moreover, Augustine and Rousseau would not have written autobiographies about their ways of life unless they had experienced some great events in their lives that made their lives worth living and therefore also worth sharing with others. In both cases one event is presented as the crucial event, the event of their lives, the event that changed their lives and made their lives worth living. That event, in each case, constituted a substantial change. That substantial change is real constitutes, in turn, a challenge to us.

Additional preliminary evidence strengthens the case for the comparison of the two authors. Even a glance—the details will follow—at the two scenes is illuminating. Both men are in the grip of contradictions within them as formed and informed by their "head" and "heart." Both men are acutely aware of their death and are ill. Both men are aware of others who have resolved their difficulty by a substantial change in them. Both men walk alone in self-dissatisfaction to a solitary place. Both men experience chance or what appears as chance in relation to their contradictory state.. By chance both men read in silence something that relates directly to their predicament. Both men are gifted by something that does not originate by their own efforts. Neither of them envisions himself as an autonomous self. Both men fall under a tree and exhibit non-verbal utterances surrounding or during the event. Both men experience the event of their lives: substantial change. Both men turn, are born again, to a new life. Both men become wise. Both men meet with a friend to tell of the great event. Both friendships are altered. Both men live the rest of their lives in the attempt to live towards or in the truth experienced in the event. Both men face tests, become authors, including authors of autobiography, because of the event of their lives, to which I therefore now turn.

1

Before his "Conversion" to God by God by means of His supra-natural, supra-rational, unearned "gift" of grace, rooted in divine particular providence, we find Augustine in the following circumstances, internal and external. He is intellectually convinced—a sort of certainty—that the incarnation is the truth. It is the true solution to a kind of dualism: the dualism of good and evil. Incarnation, in turn, presupposes the Fall; and the Fall means that death is certain for man and therefore for him. Death means eternal afterlife for good or ill: unimaginable bliss with God and others or unendurable enduring suffering, eternal damnation. The former is possible because of the incarnation and the latter is a consequence of sin, or even error, since the latter is rooted in the former: the undue love of worldly goods. Of the latter, lust (or natural eros) constitutes Augustine's specific problem. Augustine is especially impressed by the anti-natural, anti-erotic aspects of the life of Jesus: sexual abstinence and resurrection, not to mention virgin birth. In particular, he cannot be certain that his particular form of sin, intense sexual passion, will not render him subject to eternal damnation. Hence, he "dreads" his death (B. 120, 135–136,154).

Augustine's certainty of incarnation is the root of his problem. On the one hand, God commands him to love Him purely: with all his heart, mind and soul. On the other hand, given the Fall, this is an impossible moral demand. And his lust is such that, as we will see, absent the "gift" of grace, he must live a life that can be characterized, to say the least, as between a sort of serial and cyclical reluctant continence and incontinence.

To be bit more specific, Augustine is in the grip of contradictory loves: of lust and of God. His "heart" is at war, torn in diametrically opposed directions. And his "head" sides with one of his loves, God; yet he is also convinced of the incarnation and hence that lust is a great sin. His very identity, as formed and informed by his heart and his head, is in a contradictory state. He is plagued by his awareness of his dread of death in this state and of his self-repulsion or self-hatred.

His unhappy self-consciousness is exacerbated by the fact that he is aware that his "head" can command him to walk but that he is not able to rule himself in relation to his natural eros or lust (B. 133, 151). As we will soon see, he is not yet in a psychological condition to "leap," to obey, to submit in child-like obedience, on the model of "little ones" that sometimes surround Christ, to the comands of God (B. 135, 139, 144).

For now, he is in a state of perplexing paralysis: rather than certain of the incarnation and its presupposition and implications; in the grip of natural eros; in fear and love of God; and in dread of death and eternal damnation. Augustine is in a real bind.

By chance he experiences hearsay of the fate of others similarly situated. This experience will intensify his contradictory state and bring him to the brink of his "leap" (B.155). He hears stories about others who loved various worldly goods. Nevertheless, God turned them to Him and they found their way to salvation. He must be especially alert to hear lustful stories, as well as those about the other worldly goods of power, wealth, and gluttony. For his, and perhaps our, good or ill, lustful stories are not forthcoming. It is therefore worth noting what is said in this regard. Understandably, Augustine is especially impressed by one hearsay or story. He is especially struck by the post-conversion deeds of literal and, perhaps, also virtual castration for the sake of the kingdom of God(B. 138).

Be this as it may, chance hearsay of the conversion of others to more effective obedience to God's commands has an important effect on Augustine. If this substantial change can happen to others perhaps it can happen to him. Simultaneously encouraged and shamed, hopeful and fearful for his fate, his awareness of the contradictions within him is heightened as they are deepened and tightened. They come to head as a preparation for his "leap" from his present state as "hanging." (B. 154, 155).

Again by chance, Augustine finds himself in a Garden with fig trees. He has retreated there to weep alone in self-loathing. He falls in anguish under a fig tree. By chance his situation is akin to the Garden of Eden and the fall, rooted in disobedience to the command of God and the consequences of that disobedience. By chance he hears a command, but he cannot see its source. It is the voice a child. He cannot tell the gender of the child. The command comes from a sort of genderless one, a non-erotic one, akin to the aforementioned "little ones" who sometimes surround Christ and whom he praises, as well as akin to eunuchs. He cannot tell to whom the voice is directed. Could it be to a parent or adult by a child? He also has never heard the content of the voice before, at least from a child. The speech is cast in the form of a chanted command, stated at least twice for emphasis. The chance command chanted by the child is clear: "Pick up and read. Pick up and read." The chant temporarily diverts his attention away from his despair. He takes the command from the child to be to him. He, an adult, is about to obey the command of a child. He cannot obey the hearsay of adults, even hearsay about Christ. He cannot even obey himself. He cannot rule himself in relation to his lust, but he is about to obey the commands of a child. By chance there is something to read nearby. In response to the command of the child he is able to command himself to walk to the Bible. He flips it open by chance to a page and paragraph. He reads the following most important hearsay, hearsay from another who heard that it was said by Jesus and converted. He reads in silence the following crucial command related to his perplexed state: "Not in...debauchery and lewdness...but put on the Lord Jesus Christ...and make no provision for the flesh or the gratification of your desires" (B.157)

This written hearsay is radically different than all the rest. It is suffused with divine action, supra-natural, supra-rational divine action. This miraculous event entails a divine "gift," the all-important gift of the loving grace of God. The effect of this cause is supranatural substantial change: Augustine's "Conversion" to God. Finally, he is somehow able to "leap" to greet God (B. 155). Augustine is born again (B. 139–140). He is given that which he neither deserves nor can earn. The contradictions within him, rooted in his head and his heart, are resolved or relieved by God. In particular, his lust is dissolved or attenuated as he is informed by God's supra-natural wholly other-regarded love, the opposite of natural eros, which is self-regarded and needy. Christian love, via God, must be wholly other-regarded or God's love of us and our love of others through God's love of us would be self-regarding love and hence God himself would be erotic or needy and hence defective.

To continue, Augustine is reborn to wisdom, wisdom of God: as the beginning of wisdom is fear of God so its end is veneration or awe of God. Augustine abandons prideful merely human wisdom, philosophy, and as we will soon see, pursues understanding of supra-rational miracles, rooted in his new supra-natural God given faith. Natural inequalities of mind, especially strengths of mind—and Augustine had substantial powers of mind—pale into near insignificance and are of no consequence in the eyes of God and in the face of spiritual inequality. More importantly, the chain of lust, sexual bondage, is broken or weakened. God, who can harden the hearts of men to Him for His purposes, can certainly break or weaken a humanly hardened lust and fill our hearts with His love of us to strengthen our merely human love of Him and therefore our love of others, that which no one can either deserve or earn. And since, except for absolutely keeping his promises, for our good or ill, his "ways" are not ours, "He will be Gracious to whom He will be Gracious," the proper translation of His name as, "I am who I am," therefore means "I shall Be who I shall Be" (B.128).[3] Augustine will have to struggle with this notion of spiritual inequality among men and its implication of predetermination.

---

3   If we did not have reason we could not understand the commands of God. That God is the unity of reason and love or will and that His reason is above our reason, supra-rational reason, can only be rooted in an act of faith by us since who He is, how He can be Who and What he is, and what He says and does cannot always or even typically be fully accessed by our reason. If it could we would need faith.

Be that as it may, on the basis of his personal experience of God, not human hearsay strictly speaking, he now sees his past in a different light. All of the events that he had experienced as chance were exposed for what they are: illusion. These events, perhaps all events, are in truth caused by divine particular providence. What is more, death is overcome and eternal damnation may not be his likely fate. If he passes the test of Final Judgment he will enter into an eternal life of bliss with God and others. His dread of death is dissolved or at least weakened as his love of God is requited by God. Above all, Augustine is a requited lover.

After his "Conversion" Augustine meets his friend who also converts. Their friendship is deepened. Both go off to a joyous, perhaps even tearful, celebration with Augustine's mother.

Augustine comes to see that chance, death, and contradiction are ultimately illusions in the face of divine particular providence, and, derivatively, to understand his and mankind's need for divine rule or guidance. He responds to his "Conversion" by dedicating his life to Christ. He lives to bring glory to God, not to himself. He devotes himself to the study of the Bible and to sermons. In particular, he dedicates himself to his faith, faith seeking understanding of the supra-rational, supra-natural truths. Specifically, for present purposes, it is important to note that since the City of is real and hence the final solution to Plato's problem of the chance combination of contradictories—wisdom and politics—that problem is merely a secondary problem for Augustine. He is not, strictly speaking, a political philosopher. Rather, he is a political theologian who merely had to apply and teach others in the future to apply the standards of life in the City of God to the particular intersections of that City to his and their particular political circumstances. After all, cities do not save souls. Hence he must reject the primacy of the political for human good or ill.

Faith seeking understanding, especially self-knowledge, is not without its difficulties for Augustine. To know ourselves we must know God. But, of course, to say the least, God as such cannot be fully known. Otherwise, there would be no place for faith or trust. And though the command of God is to love Him with all our heart, mind, and soul, it is an impossible moral demand for fallen man. What is more, since only God can know our heart, full self-knowledge is also impossible. The unity of the natural and the divine supra-natural, supra-rational in Augustine must remain to him an inaccessible miracle. Moreover, ultimately God not Augustine must be his final judge.

2

Whereas Augustine's problem stems from the distinction, meaning, and relation of the natural and the supra-natural, Rousseau's is rooted in the same categories, but with regard to the "needs of nature" and "those of opinion" (K.575, 580).[4] Whereas Augustine demotes nature in light of the supra-natural, Rousseau resurrects nature as good. On the whole nature is good and humankind as a part of nature is naturally good. As will be shown, this difference between them applies especially to natural eros, properly ordered.

Before his "Illumination" we find Rousseau in the following situation. Naturally born by chance, his birth caused the death of his mother by chance. Naturally born frail and ill, he is facing a death sentence according to doctors. Nature, including chance will loom large in Rousseau's world. As with Augustine, Rousseau's understanding of death will also prove crucial to his self-knowledge. Immediately before his enlightenment, he is also in the prime of his

---

4   As we will see, embodied awareness of self aware of other does not mean neutral observation precisely because we are embodied. The embodied self that is loved is either mainly loved as in accordance with one's own nature or as loved by others. The analytic difference has a common root: to be loved. Even self hatred is good if experienced as bad and leads one towards natural goodness. The standards of self esteem are indeed very high: to be aware that one is truly a lover, and even a knower, of the truth by means of great tests that one must pass. G.218n. XV.163:8. See especially G. 187: 57 on "play acting" as opposed to seeking self-knowledge. Most humans most of the time must put on public masks that gradually become who they erroneously think they are.

life as a poor "nobody" (K.291). He must find a way to make living and live a way appropriate to his nature. And the love of himself as loved by others, as a requited lover, will prove, as opposed to Augustine, to be a key aspect of his lack of self-knowledge. He, as opposed to Augustine, must learn to love himself as an unrequited lover, a Solitary Walker.

Less generally, before his "Illumination" we find that Rousseau is out of place and out of sorts: like Augustine he is in self-contradiction. After his enlightenment we find that he has discovered that his place is to be out of place in order to seek and maintain self-knowledge. More specifically, and in the same language as Augustine, Rousseau's, as formed and informed by his "heart" and his "head," is torn in diametrically opposed directions. But unlike Augustine, his self-contradictions stem from a lack of self-knowledge regarding the "needs of nature" and the needs of "opinion," including especially "false opinion," rooted in the political domain. (K. 573, 575, 580, 586. See "false opinion," K. 576)

On the side of nature, we find that he was "born with a natural love of solitude." Complete solitude will prove incompatible with self-knowledge. To his natural love of solitude is added a natural "talent," a natural not a supra-natural "gift," of a very strong mind, especially including—and this will prove to be a problem for him—imagination, the power to image. The two "naturals" converge to constitute a life primarily oriented upon solitary contemplation, the love of himself as living the life of the mind. In particular, solitude is for the sake of his "spirit of freedom," freedom from the "active life." The active life, in turn, is life in relation to others, the life of duties, especially "civic duties," as well as of deeds as such, even including the thought-deeds of speech and writing. It is important to note in this regard that the spirit of freedom from duties to others includes freedom even from due gratitude, but that this spirit is not rooted in "pride:" hatred of the recognition of dependence on others; or contempt of the active life as undignified. It is simply that such things run against the grain of that which he loves. The spirit of freedom from the active life, in turn, is freedom for the sake of reading and the contemplation of that which he reads. Freedom is for the life of the mind. Given his "talents," this way of life requires the "least" effort on his part and renders him a self-proclaimed unbelievably "lazy" good for nothing from the perspective of the active life. As we will see, this way of life proves ultimately inadequate for self-knowledge. (K.573–573, 580; G.158:49)

That which Rousseau contemplates, in turn, renders him one of "heroic and romantic tastes," in the following sense of the terms. He finds his "enjoyment" in the contemplation of great heroes and lovers, based on Plutarch and novels. To foreshadow a bit, Rousseau will become aware, enlightened to the truth, that Plutarch, like so many events in his life actually "fell into his hands"—the same word, "fell," used in his "Illumination" scene—by chance. A condition of his contemplation is chance. As we will soon see, he also loves certainty, another condition of his contemplative life. But certainty and chance are contradictory. To continue, he populates his intelligent imagination with these "chimerical beings" and they are the "social circle" with whom he communes in solitude (K. 572–574).However, the life of the mind is complicated in that it is also to his "advantage."

Advantage, in turn, refers to relations with others. It means that the life of contemplation is a life of the "least risk" and "the most reliable as I *needed* it to be." This love of the reliable or certain refers to the conditions, not the contents, of contemplation. It refers to the security and comfort of the "charm of the study" in which he can read what he wants and conjure up what contemplates at will. (K. 572, 575–575; G. 99:25). This certainty of the conditions of possibility of contemplation, this need or love of the reliable or certain will ultimately be recognized by him as a need of "opinion" not a "need of nature." This need, in turn, will also find its way into the next stage of his quest for self-knowledge. For now, we discover that this need informs his awareness of his discontent with his contradictory self, to which I now turn.

The conditions and the contents of contemplation are also in contradiction and he is more or less aware of this truth about himself. He is an actionless lover of action figures; an unheroic lover of heroes; an asocial lover of social beings; a risk-free lover of risk-takers. Those he contemplates live the active life and presupposes the social and political life; life lived on the plane or domain of deeds, precisely that which he frees himself from in order to flee to contemplate. What is more, unless action figures, as heroes, accept the love of just anybody, it would be indeed odd if they, as members of his "social circle" with which he communes, would requite the love of this lazy good-for-nothing who, as such, would not even write about them!

To foreshadow, Rousseau's romantic hero-worship will come to be seen by him to be-speak a semi-secret love of himself as loved by others as do the heroes he contemplates. This kind of love of himself as imaginary hero contradicts his love of solitude. Hence, as we will see, he also has a love of society, but that love too will prove to be a need of "opinion": he loves society only to the extent it requites his love. Ultimately, as we will see, he loves the human species and himself as its peak.

To continue, his "heart" is torn. He loves contradictory goods. He loves himself as solitary and himself as loved by others. What is more, his "head" contradicts one aspect of his "heart:" He has "reasons to hate society." The two reasons are, first, that his contemporary society does not recognize or love him for his place in it as solitary contemplator; and, second, that his society does not live up the standards of the lives led by those in his imaginary social circle. The problems in his embodied psychic life are clear. The heroes he contemplates are at least twice removed and romanticized, even by the hearsay he reads, from the lives they actually led. More importantly, his way of life contradicts the standard he uses to hate his society. And he hates society because it does not requite his love (K. 575; G. 4:8–9, 19:44, 94:9, 99:24).[5] As we will soon see, hate is

5   A key root of the love of certainty is political society. G: 8:14. Certainty and the needs of the body go together. For instance, it is understandable that one would not want to be so ignorant of nature that one would unknowingly eat a hemlock omelet. On the problem natural nourishment by the "acorn," see note 7 below.

rooted in unrequited love, just as the love of oneself as loved by others is rooted in and a modification of simple love of oneself alone.

As we will soon see, two consequences of his enlightenment will be his discovery of "What I had to do (become 'active') for myself and what I had to think (not 'hate') about my fellows." Both discoveries will contribute to his insight that the contradictions within himself are in truth contradictions between himself and society, especially political society (K.573, 574, 576).

When Rousseau adds to that which he contemplates the "celestial intelligences" (including Bacon, Descartes, Newton, and the like) that founded, for the "greater glory of philosophy," the emerging dispensation in his century—he is ripe and ready to see the possible resolutions of his self-contradictions. The shift from romanticism to scientism, as contradictory as these two appear, has a common root. The founders of political philosophy, understood as the politicization of philosophy, became the heroes of his new social circle. He saw them as solitary contemplators like himself. To contemplate these heroes was not in contradiction with the conditions of contemplation. What is more, they were Heroes of the Truth! They were "wise" men. He will discover that just as they were the Heroes of the Truth of his century so he was "seduced" by and therefore "subjected" to the "opinions" of his century, taken as true. To love oneself as loved by others can mean subjection to others, to the opinion of others. To love requited love can enslave one to the beloved, like Voltaire, for instance. To continue, the truths they contemplated combined the "reliable" or the certainty of the conditions of contemplation that Rousseau "needed" with the contents of contemplation. The new objects of contemplation are not action figures but figures of action or motion. They are doubly abstract mathematical formulas of matter in motion. Hence, demonstrable "proof" means truth: knowledge is certainty. Chance is an illusion. Rousseau will come to see that this vision of chance is an error and hence the cause of evil. For now, for Rousseau, to the risk-free life is added the prospect of the error-free life of certainty. He maintains his love of certainty on the plane of the conditions of contemplations and adds to them the certainty of the objects of contemplation: the certainty of the truth or truths. The existence of the objects of contemplation, in turn, justifies the contemplative way of life, the life of the mind (K.579, G. 109:8; 94–95: 9, 99:24).

This vision, called later a "youthful division," also held forth the promise of the resolution of his love of himself as solitary contemplator and his love of himself as loved by others. Since that which can be known are necessities, they are "reliable" or predictable. As such, they are controllable for human good. Man can intervene into the causal chain and alter its dangerous effects. Not only is chance an illusion but even death can be overcome. A man-made Garden of Eden of universal peace, plenty, health, bodily immortality, even the imperishability of the human species, is possible. Hence, the Heroes of the Truth are also the great, God-like, benefactors of mankind. They deserve and will receive the immortality of their names in the immortal "." Given his talents, Rousseau envisions himself as their equal. He will join them in that Republic. His love of himself as a lover and knower of the truth and his love of himself as loved by others are now in harmony, not contradiction (G. 94:9; 4:2, 100:27). There is only one great problem with this resolution, to which I now turn.

All that Rousseau must now do is a deed. He must abandon the inactive live. He must, like his heroes, execute the thought-deed. He must become an author. He must at least begin to make a name for himself. He must begin to contribute to the politicization of philosophy in its enlightenment component. However, he fails to do the deed. He cannot publish. His love of himself as loved by others is so strong that it trumps his love of himself as lover and knower of the truth, as he sees it. He lacks the requisite courage, rooted in love, to risk public ridicule and scorn. He fears shame more than he loves the truth, as he now sees it. I now note that the publication at issue was his *Narcissus, or the Lover of Himself*, the play which, as we will soon see, he finally had the philosophical courage to publish after his "Illumination" and after he overcame shame, the enemy of self-knowledge. (B. G. 92:106 and note 42 below).

It is crucial to recognize that his vision at this time and his failure to publish contributed to his progress in self-knowledge. After all, he did become a lover of the truth, an important step towards self-knowledge. Given his enlightenment, the contents of the truth will radically change. And he is now more acutely aware of the contradiction between his love of himself in solitary contemplation and his love of himself as loved by others. He will soon have the philosophical courage to "make his talents known," his version of Augustine's "leap," as he discovers the truth for himself, as opposed to by hearsay. In the meantime, since "wise men" study, he retreats to the reliable conditions of contemplation and the apparently risk-free life of the mind. Given his "illumination," Rousseau's retreat from the active life will also constitute further progress in self-knowledge. He spends "much time"—twenty years—in intense "researches" into the great books, and perhaps more importantly, engages in "much reflection and much observation." Perhaps most importantly he discovers *esoteric writing* by ancients and moderns. It causes a "great blow" to his reading of some of the great books and his understanding of his past heroes, especially Cicero. As opposed to Augustine, Rousseau must earn his "Illumination" by "philosophizing," on his own. This time turned out to be mainly the preparation required to take full advantage of the "good fortune" of his "Illumination"; the time of his exercise and activation of his natural potentials that made him ready for the event that "rid himself of all this vain scientific pomp;" made him ready for his moment, his enlightenment moment, to which we are now prepared to turn our attention (K. 572, 579, 295, 279, 642n 11, 18; G. 42:39n).[6]

---

6   Philosophy proper is to "philosophize." G. 48:55n. False philosophers are "the philosopher," including "philosophasters," and "half philosophers." G. 99: 23, 210:8. "Philosophy is the farthest thing from war and sacred rights." The latter two are united in the notion of sacrifice! G.103:34n. On Rousseau and esoteric writing, see K. The History of this Fatal doctrine: Rousseau and the Background of the "Interior Doctrine." SVEC. Rousseau and the Philosophers. Volume: SVEC 2010:12., Series editor: Jonathan Mallinson. Volume editor: Michael O'Dea.

3

As noted, Rousseau speaks of his "Illumination" in language similar to Augustine's account of his "Conversion." I now note, by way of a general introduction, language of Rousseau that also and even more clearly begs for comparison with Augustine. First, according to Rousseau and in the hypothetical, "If" there is anything "akin to a sudden inspiration" it is his "Illumination." It is the cause of a complete "pause" in his life, a pause such that he cannot remember, even confuses, how long it lasted. It is as though he entered a sort of timeless transcendent present. Second, and again in the hypothetical, "If" his life is "eternal," then his enlightenment would always be "present" to him forever. This means that even if he is not eternal—which proves to be his opinion—this present pause in his life, this transcendent present, will be present to him as long as he lives. Third, it produced an "inconceivable motion" in him that brought together his head and his heart. This motion is neither a divine motion, as in the "Conversion" of Augustine by the action of God, nor the motion conceived of by the modern science of his time, according to which motion is wholly conceivable (K. 575, 293, 295).

Less generally, the whole "Illumination" scene is surrounded by chance events: from the "unforeseen," to the "Illumination" itself as "good fortune." Between the former and the latter we find a sort of dance of prudence and chance. And after the former we find prudence oriented upon "What (he) had to do for himself," namely, achieve "full self-knowledge." Self-rule by prudence and self-knowledge go together and are opposed to divine guidance or rule and particular providence. After I present the immediate context and the content of Rousseau's enlightenment, I will proceed to attempt to account for the important and interesting gap between his "Illumination" and his well-earned achievement of "full self-knowledge." (K. 241, 291–292; G.94–95:9, 105:39)

Rousseau's "friend," Diderot, affectionately nicknamed, "the philosopher," is in jail for his publication of an enlightenment piece without using, as was the custom, a pseudonym. He is in the grip of the theological-political problem for the philosophers of his century: persecution. This problem is on Rousseau's mind: to become an author is that about which he was "thinking the least" (K. 575). He is and may remain, as stated earlier, a "nobody." As noted he is also in his natural prime facing death by illness. Whether nature is neutral or hostile to man is definitely on his mind. More specifically, Rousseau visits Diderot when he can, usually every other day in the company of Diderot's wife. They go together in her cab. They are not as poor as Rousseau and, by the way, Diderot owes Rousseau money that he never pays back. This fact may account, at least in part, for Rousseau's visits and account for why, even before his "Illumination," Rousseau was inclined to turn his face: his "head almost turned" from him (K. 292). However that may be, this time, by chance, Rousseau must go alone, as a solitary walker. He cannot afford a cab. The walk is two leagues long. When he had to go alone before, he prudently picked up by chance something to glance at to slow or moderate his pace. This time it is by chance very hot. Is nature good? Given the heat, his illness, and the distance, he, again, prudently picks up something by chance to read in order, again, to moderate his pace. He is unaware of it, but the readable just happens to be *The Mercury of France* in which resides a question posed by an Academy to address for a Prize, including money.

By "custom" or "opinion," most of the trees along the way to the jail have been pruned. If not, there would be shade by nature to ease his trip. The relation of nature and opinion, the "needs of nature 'and the needs "of opinion," is also on his mind. Tiring and overheating, he prudently looks for shade. By chance he sees a shady oak tree. He rests in its shade. Just as the Fig tree in relation to Augustine's "Conversion" clearly represents the Garden of Eden, so the "oak tree" is an obvious reference to nature, nature as good in a certain sense, nature as change as growth accounted for or described as the activation of natural potential. As we will soon see, given his enlightenment, his past way of life constituted the exercise of his natural talents, his being at work, activating his natural potentials of mind and soul, in preparation, in hindsight, for the upcoming event of his life.

Rousseau now *picks up* the paper to read in solitary silence and, like Augustine, flips to a page and glances at a paragraph. As Plutarch's book fell into his hands by chance, so too does this readable. The contrast between what Rousseau reads in solitary silence and what Augustine reads could hardly be greater. Whereas Augustine reads a divine command, Rousseau reads a question, a question of a human not divine origin. It is "one of the grand and finest questions ever raised," namely: "Has the Restoration of the Sciences and the Arts (the so-called Renaissance, or the politicization of philosophy) contributed to the Purification of Morals?" (574, 575 K. 642n.11)[7] Upon the reading of this great question, a question which relates directly to his prior ways, as did the command to Augustine, Rousseau, falls to the ground and recounts what he experienced as follows (K.575–576; 294–295).

Rousseau does not weep, as does Augustine, but cries as a newborn baby and then, afterwards, laughs at his prior dead self. Augustine never laughs in this way, especially at himself. Rousseau "became another man" as his prior self dies. He no longer loves or thinks what he did before. He, like Augustine, is born again. Unlike Augustine who experienced supra-natural substantial change, Rousseau goes through natural substantial change, a metamorphosis, like that which occurs to a butterfly, or better, a cicada. It is cast in the language of natural growth from "simplicity" to complexity. It is akin to the oak he is under in relation to his own natural potentials, even though, as shown, our natural potentials are not actualized without our effort. Above all, he learns "What [he] had to do for [himself] and to think about [his] fellows." Hence, I

---

7   The Oak tree looms large or stands tall in Rousseau's world. It is the tree of both life and knowledge. His whole system is in its image of which he begins by only showing its "trunk." G. 134:2, 147:29, 110:9. Rousseau's whole corpus is a heterogeneous whole about the natural heterogeneous whole. See note 13 below. Whereas, Augustine is repulsed by natural generation and decay, for Rousseau they are necessary for the whole notion of activity that activates natural potential, a or the key truth for him(B. 142).

now turn to the contents of his "Illumination," the "great truths" which led to this conclusion (K. 575, 294, 580: G. 94–95:9 esp. n.; G. 25: 27,170:26).[8]

A. Chance

First, since his enlightenment as whole occurred by chance, called by him "good fortune," a key content of his "Illumination" is the reality of chance. He finally becomes fully aware of the full reality of chance. Every one of the past effects of chance on his life is now clear to him, impressed on his mind. That which became an illusion in the face of divine particular providence for Augustine, as well as for the young Rousseau in the face of natural necessity, is real. As such, reality is supra-rational but not supra-natural. What is more, chance death at any instant is real and the death of his prior self is but the beginning of true self-knowledge which requires learning how to die or is preparation for dying and being dead. And for Rousseau, as opposed to Augustine, to die is to simply cease "to be." (G. 137:8). Just as he is a "nobody" so he will ultimately become completely unknowable. As we will soon see, nothing is eternal. Love of eternity is loves illusion. As chance is real, so certainty is a need of opinion not a need of nature (G. 94:9; K. 294–295). These causes of Rousseau's contradictory self are resolved or relieved.

Chance is also the source of his natural "gifts," his strong natural potentials, especially of mind, which only he can actualize as natural potentials, but which are not predictable or inheritable in a predictable manner. These natural "gifts," not the supra-natural "gift" of "grace," are the necessary conditions of possibility of an effective search for self-knowledge. Moreover, not spiritual inequality, but natural inequality of mind, especially prudence or

8   Evidently, the embodied self or identity or ego is the very important seat of human experience. See his wonderful attempt to describe the natural trans-rational being of the beings. K. 572. On the irreducible complexity of nature, see note 7 above and 21 below.

dialectic and natural inequality of soul, or eros, will prove, as we will now see, crucial in Rousseau's new-found world (G.131–132, 158, 49).[9]

B. Contradiction

Second, not only chance, but also natural contradiction is an element of Rousseau's new-found insights. Contradiction and chance go together. The latter is caused by the former, but for present purposes both are natural but supra-rational. Natural contradiction, in turn, will prove to be the root of natural transcendent "mysteries," as opposed to supra-natural, supra-rational, "miracles." Enduring, if not eternal, *mystery* and *miracle* are contradictories. The complexity of nature provides the opportunity for natural transcendence within nature itself. More specifically, Rousseau discovers for himself the "contradiction in the social system," especially in political society, as such. The disproportion or contradiction between the politicization of philosophy and political society proper, so well articulated by him in his *First Discourse,* is deepened to include the contradiction within the human species between the "true" or "genuine" philosopher, as opposed to former "half" philosophers and political society. On the one hand, the political, as such, originates out of the needs of the body and is for the sake of great deeds, especially the courageous speechless deed of death, rooted in the love of country and visa-versa. Great political speeches—encomiums and funeral orations—surround and are for this great speechless deed. However, the political, as such, exits in the element of "opinion," especially about God or gods, taken as true. It is Plato's cave. The

9   See also G. 197:n.IX. On whether human life is a rather poor natural "gift" and when, for most, it is not good and therefore not worth living, see G. 97, Note IX: 1 and 201:6. See also C. Kelly. Rousseau and the Bad Calculations of the Philosophers, SVEC. Rousseau and the Philosophers. Volume SVEC. 2010:12. Series Editor: Jonathan Mallinson. Volume Editor: Michael O'Dea.

needs of the body, the needs of the mind, especially for order, the atmosphere in which the latter operates, are amplified into the need for certainty and converge on the side of the needs of "opinion." The need for certainty is rooted in the political domain, for instance, that the unjust will not ultimately flourish and the just will flourish because God is just; that mutual trust and not suspicion prevail among citizens. Mutually suspicious, untrustworthy, citizens are unhappy citizens, bad citizens, and especially bad soldiers. Again, this element within Rousseau's contradictory self is resolved. As we will see, the true or genuine philosopher assumes the priority of thought to deeds. Deeds, including the thought-deeds of speech and writing, are for the sake of thought oriented upon the truth, self-knowledge, not opinion or false opinion (K. 579; G. 17,131:2; G. 7:11, 101:30n.; G.6:9, 28:61, 12:75, G. 6).

Both of these contradictions, in turn, are rooted in the contradiction within the human species: natural inequality in mind and soul. The naturally strong in mind are to the naturally weak in mind as a giant is to a dwarf (consider reproduction for the species), celestial intelligence to us, adult to child, the wise to imbecile, and the solitary to the herd. He wonders if they are of the same species (G. 158:48, 188:56, 203–204:13–14,141:17; G. 8:13).[10] This truth resolves another component of Rousseau contradictory self. To hate society, including the naturally weak in mind, would be to hate the truth. This is a hard and, perhaps, sad,

10 "Children should be left some baubles" G. 31:11. He properly wonders if they are fully the same species. G. 140–141:16. Though a "herd" they are unlike "cattle" since they possess speech. G. 8:13, 18: 41. Perhaps this is why Rousseau calls his whole system "sad and great," and "true but distressing." G. 108–109: 6–7. In this regard, see G. 141:17; K. 529, G.88:9, 102. See L. Sorenson. "Natural Inequality and Rousseau's Political Philosophy in His Discourse on Inequality." *The Western Political Quarterly*. Vol. 43. no.41. 1990. 763–788; and "Rousseau's Authorial Voices in His Dedication of His Discourse on Inequality to the Republic of Geneva." History of Political Thought. Vol. 30. n. 3. 2009.

but not hateful, truth. For Rousseau, natural inequality in mind replaces the spiritual inequality indicated by Augustine. Natural inequality of soul, in turn, refers to the intensity and objects of love, need or eros.

Embodied eros is the first cause of all human action, internal and external. Love is oriented upon one's own well being, good or happiness. At its best, natural love, as opposed to love rooted in the needs of opinion, seeks its good, with the least possible harm, or greatest possible good, to others. Natural eros is never other-regarded, except in its modified form: the love of others to the extent they requite one's love. Just as the "soul insensitively proportions itself to the objects that occupy it," so the hierarchy of objects determines the natural hierarchy of souls. The natural strength or intensity of the soul is crucial. Strong embodied eros overcomes all "obstacles" to its objects. And it makes it possible for one to resist the "current" or "tide" of one's century. It hunts. It stalks. It will not take no for an answer. As the truth, not glory and honor, is highest object, so the true lover of the truth is the peak of the human species. The other "needs of nature" are nourishment and sex. Since the truths, including chance, contradiction, and hence natural inequality, are impersonal truths which do not requite our love of them, it follows that Rousseau, as opposed to Augustine, must "learn to live" as an unrequited lover himself as a lover and knower of the impersonal truths, truths that do not requite their lover. Hence, a key component of his prior contradictory self— his love of himself as loved by others—is resolved or relieved. He must, and will, as we will soon see, "learn to live without the esteem of others" (G. 156:45, 163:8, 154:38, 27:59; G. 103, 12:26; G. 23–24:54, 92:2 95:9, 88:9).

Moreover, those who have the good fortune to combine natural strength of mind and soul, "sublime genius" or celestial intelligence and a "privileged soul," are the peak of mankind, the most excellent specimens of the human species. Hence, as the world is for man, so the whole human race is ultimately for and called to the "enlightenment and happiness of celestial intelligences" (G.

203,172,102; K. 579).[11] The latter, in turn, look up to, love, and admire nature as at least the source of their great natural gifts. As we will soon see, Nature deserves the name God. In short, Rousseau replaces "Until Christ be Formed in You" with "Until Nature is formed in You."

The contradiction of natural inequality among men also has crucial political implications. First, one who would quest for self-knowledge depends upon the political domain not only for domestic peace, the division of labor, and so on, but also as providing an atmosphere of opinion taken as true and certain, especially about God or gods, as an atmosphere in which to "test" natural strengths of mind and soul in the attempt to transcend the cave and to contact the transcendent impersonal truths, even or especially the truth about the political domain, as such. The quest through the earthly city, which seduces and subjects its denizens, for the best city is necessary in order to lead to the quest for the best man. Second, the political is ultimately for the sake of the search for knowledge, self-knowledge. Political philosophy understood as the politicization of philosophy or science useful for politics is an evil, rooted in error, caused by love's illusion. Given the truths, stated above, its Founders put forth the promise of new Garden of Eden on earth, even the immortality of the species as a means, unscrupulous means, to their own glory. The species must be immortal if their names are to be immortal. This dispensation leads to "tyranny over nature and human nature." Properly understood, the political is

11 A major, even central, purpose of the Discourse on Inequality is to account for how the "naturally strong," especially in mind, ever came to "resolve to serve the naturally weak," especially in mind, that is, politicize philosophy. G. 131: 2–4. See the point of transition, G.170:27. The politicization of philosophy was "grand and beautiful" in relation to the dark ages, a state "worse than ignorance," but was not true or good G. 6:7, 40:33. Though the "path" to the "return" to root thinking in "common sense," the "precious spoils" of the Greeks, was opened, it failed to take this step or path. G.6:7–8, 101: 29. Another revolution is needed to bring men back to common sense. G. 90: 11. Yet see 51:62.

for the sake of philosophy. For instance, the political should aid the "genuine" or "true philosopher" to employ experiments to help clarify the true nature of man, experiments that would constitute sin from the point of view of Augustine. As we will soon see, Rousseau will perform his own "great tests" on political society in order to achieve "full self-knowledge." Third, whereas the God of Augustine renders chance an illusion, and hence the chance combination of contradictories, wisdom and politics—alluded to by Plato as impossible, or highly unlikely, or, perhaps, even undesirable—is resolved by the reality of the City of God; so Rousseau weighs in with his own contribution to the issue. Rousseau's city in speech, his *Social Contract,* most fundamentally proposes a city based on direct popular sovereignty, not chance or lot. Hence, one-half of the problem of chance is resolved. If, by chance, a potential philosopher is born in this city, then this natural-born citizen would also be sovereign, a member of the sovereign. Fourth, and lastly, Rousseau saw the "abuse" of our "institutions" which means rule for the good for the ruler instead of the ruled. He attempted to address this problem—to square a circle—in his *Social Contract.* Consideration of chance and of contradiction leads to the third component of Rousseau's "Illumination," or insight (G. 94:5, 141:17, 125:4).[12]

C. Natural Mystery

Third, Rousseau "saw another universe." The universe or whole is not as Rousseau thought as a youth, or young man. It is not rational and suffused with the truth of certainty. It is not reducible to matter in mechanical motion. The whole is not rational. It transcends reason. The whole is a "heterogeneous whole," that entails parts, which, in turn, are also heterogeneous wholes, including, as shown, the human species, and, as will be

12 See the beginning and end of the Social Contract and especially H. Gildin. Rousseau's Social Contract, The Design of the Argument. The University of Chicago Press. 1983.

shown, each human being, and all things, right down to the smallest entity. Contradiction resides in the nature of all things. The whole is greater than the sum of, and produces, the parts it then depends upon. The stability or equilibrium of the whole is produced by its conflicting, contradictory, parts. This, of course, means that "the truth has only one way of being," the way of natural "mystery." Further, if that with parts must fall apart, the conclusion of experience, then the whole is subject to disintegration. The whole, then, is not eternal. Nothing is eternal. The contrast with Augustine, or for that matter Descartes, could not be greater. As for the former, everything depends upon, is contingent upon, the eternal God and upon the supra-natural "miracle" of incarnation. Rousseau replaces "miracle" with natural "mystery," rooted in natural contradiction. The real transcends the principle of non-contradiction. In particular, the "abyss of philosophy" is the reality of the contradictory unity called embodied mind, the evidence for which is the thought-deed, called speech or writing. All of the above leads to Rousseau's last and most fundamental insight which, given the above, might appear rather strange: "Man is naturally good" Evidently, human happiness is possible within the natural irreducible complexity of our world.[13]

13 G. xxvii; K. 577–579 and C. Kelly. Rousseau on Philosophy, Morality, and Religion. Dartmouth College Press. Hanover, New Hampshire. University Press of New England. 2007: 266 and n.27; 228, 231–233. On heterogeneous whole in relation to evil, see V. Gourevitch. Rousseau on Providence. The Review of Metaphysics. 53 (March 2000): 565–611 and J. Scott. Pride and Providence: Religion in Rousseau's Letter to Voltaire on Providence. Religion and LLnflame. Religion, Toleration and Fanaticism in the Age of Enlightenment. Mostefai, Ourida and John T. Scott. Amersteram/New York, 2009. The best account of the whole notion of heterogeneous whole is P. Stern. Knowledge and Politics in Plato's Theaetetus. Cambridge University Press. 2009. My exploration of Rousseau's view of this theme owes very much to his insightful work and above all to our invaluable conversations.

D. Natural Goodness

Fourth, "Man is naturally good." In fact, "Everything that comes from the Hands of Nature is Good." Moreover, Rousseau himself began to become a naturally good man through his "Illumination." How is one to understand these claims? To begin with, they relate to Augustine (as well as to the politicizers of philosophy). Rousseau's claims deny original sin, just as they also root evil in false opinion or error, our natural weakness, and chance. On the other hand, we find the following trajectory of argument. Since man is naturally good, nature as a whole is "justified." Evidently, since man is a part of the whole, is a natural product of the whole, and since man is naturally good, then it must follow that the whole is on the whole naturally good. How could a product or part of a whole be good if that of which it is part were bad not good? In any case, human life, rooted in the "needs of nature" not the "needs of opinion" can be a naturally good, happy life. Moreover, the point is that if Rousseau can live a naturally good life, then the natural whole, on the whole, is naturally good. Furthermore, as shown, approximations of this life may perhaps also be available to those who by nature must live in the element of "opinion," in and as denizen-citizens in a proper political society. Who could say that the courage of the citizen in the face of death for his country, rooted in his love of his country, and its love of the citizen, is not modeled on the philosophical courage, rooted in the love of the truth, which is also a preparation for death? Since all men must die, why not choose to die well?[14]

After his "Illumination," Rousseau continues his walk to the jail to visit Diderot. They meet, but the contents of Rousseau's insights, as well other matters, bode ill for the flourishing of their friendship. Just as his venture to visit Diderot in jail was a solitary

14 G. 99:24, 103n.; 101:30n; 197:n. IX, 21:49, 98–99:23. See the beginning of his *Emile*. Obviously, Rousseau may not be speaking only of his own "Hands."

walk, so Rousseau will spend the rest of his life a "Solitary Walker."[15]

4

We are now in the position to address the great question of the gap between Rousseau's "Illumination" to "great truths" and his achievement of "full self-knowledge." The beginning of the answer is that after his enlightenment Rousseau speaks of his need to see if he can make himself "consistent" with his new vision of others and the world. He has to find his way or place. He has "to make himself good for himself," become a naturally good man. What he has to think about society in general has been addressed above. But society means "his fellows" who, in turn, include his enlightenment friends, including especially Diderot, rooted, as Rousseau was before his "Illumination," in the politicization of philosophy. Rousseau, as opposed to Augustine, had to split from his enlightenment friends, and first and foremost from Diderot. What else he "had to do" for himself remains to be seen. I propose that there is a clear link between what he "had to do for" himself and his achievement of "full self-knowledge." He had to do something to achieve full self-knowledge. He had to do something to find his true place among men. He had to do something—face a "test," or "great tests," like, but radically different from, Augustine. He had to find out among whom he could "count himself" (K. 576, 580; G. 104–105:38–39). The question is, what is to be done?

Given what we already know, the conclusion of his enlightenment itself is illuminating. First, given that he is naturally inclined to solitary reading and contemplation and not the "active life," that he had to "do" anything whatsoever is noteworthy. He must abandon the life of the mind and enter active life, relate to society and, as we will see, to political society in particular. Second, the conclusion is cast in the form of a duty. He "had" to do something.

15 J.J. Rousseau, Reveries of a Solitary Walker. See also "walk alone," G. 27: 59.

But, he is especially not inclined to duties. Third, but this duty, in particular, is "for" himself. It is a duty to himself. He must do something for himself. Fourth, since all deeds, all action, is rooted in embodied eros or love of ones' own well being or good, what he must do for himself is become a naturally good man: seek his own good with the least possible harm to or greatest possible good for others. Again, what is to be done? Fifth, just as, given his enlightenment, his past constituted an ascent out of the cave of his century to the transcendent truths, even or especially the truth about the political, so to enter active life at all is to descend back into the cave.[16] As we will now see, his descent is for the sake of his own natural good, the achievement of "full self-knowledge." But again, what is to be done?

Even though before his "Illumination" he was "thinking about it the least" and it was the last thing on his mind; even though it was done almost "in spite of himself"; even though he had lacked the courage to it before—prudence dictated that he do it now. Having discovered the truths on his own, he must do it now for his own good. He finally must display his talents. He must do the thought-deed. He must take the risks of becoming an author. Prudence dictates that he publish. To publish is to participate in the cave, relate to the political. Political philosophy is not the politicization of philosophy. Political philosophy is to enter the political domain to achieve "full self-knowledge" (K. 575, 572, 580).

More specifically, as a new embodied psychic, he is as a new-born babe in the woods, in a strange new world. Evidently, it one thing to "believe" one has discovered "great things" and quite another to see if they are true and if one is naturally equipped to learn to actually live in the truth: to live as "consistent" with and in the truth. In confirmation of this account of the gap between his enlightenment and his achievement of full self-knowledge, this time

16 On the "few good," see G. 104:37, 105 n. and "entre nous" 99: n. Man is naturally good mainly because of his stance towards death, G.103–104: 35n., especially the material in Virgil before that quoted by Rousseau.

of life is called by him the time of "great tests" for the sake of self-knowledge. Evidently, the complex unity of our embodied soul is mysterious to us. It is difficult if not impossible to know precisely what we truly love. One point is rather clear: the love of one's own, especially one's own "self," however defined, is very difficult if not impossible to overcome. For instance, even after the tests are completed and he is bold enough, rooted in the love of the truth, to proclaim that his motto is "Dedicate Life to the Truth," he still wonders whether his claim may somehow also be rooted mainly in "secret amour-propre," which includes the love of oneself as loved by others.[17]

To continue, he had to publish, display his talents, make his "talents known," in order to test the truth. He must put them forth, "scribble" them, for discussion and consideration by others, to see the responses and to respond to the responses. Further, he must discover for himself if he has the strength of mind to be the proper defender, upholder, of the truth. He must also "test" his soul. Since the "soul insensitively proportions *itself* to the objects that occupy it," he must discover for himself if his soul is more or less oriented upon glory than it is upon truth, upon "loving" as well as "knowing" the truth.[18]

17 108–109: 6–7. Evidently, to "abandon" his own "self," to be possessed by his love of the truth and hence to have the philosophical courage to do so, made the abandonment of his children somewhat less difficult. He presents this notion by analogy to his play, Narcissus, or on the Lover of Himself. See "clearly enough" G. 95:9. Since life is naturally good, Rousseau, for the most part, is against abortion G. 200: 5.

18 K. 573; G. 170:26–27; G. 92:2, 101n; G. 92:2, 27:59.On Rousseau's responses see R. Masters. Rousseau and the Attacks on the First and Second Discourses. Studies of the Discourses of Rousseau. ed. Jean Terrasse. Ottawa: Pense Libre No.1. 1988. In addition to the account by Masters, I add that this was time for Rousseau to test himself for the sake of full self-knowledge. After the tests he says the following: "I will show myself...as I see myself, and as I am, for since I pass my life with myself I ought to know myself." K. 574

To be specific, the highest goal of his *First Discourse* is not the prize money, though that purpose was not insignificant. It highest purpose was to discover for himself who he really is and is not. He does so by simultaneously attacking the politicizers of philosophy and by presenting the truth about the political proper. As for the latter, he must make the best case for political man, who he is not: he resurrects Fabricius and the like. As for the former, he judged the work a success in part precisely because it "did not fail to make himself a host of enemies," among the politicizers of philosophy. How better test his prior longstanding love of himself as loved by others as it competed with his love of the truth? (K. 575; G. 92:3)[19]

He then proceeded to publish a play, *The Village Soothsayer*. It too was a great success in the opposite sense. It was acclaimed by all. It was loved and so was he. It goes without saying that it also made him much-needed money. In this regard, he was then offered a fine stipend or pension to become a state-supported playwright, an offer which he turned down in order to be free to publish whatever he wanted. As we will now see, he needed to continue to experiment to attain full self-knowledge.

His third test, his third deed of prudence, was to publish the very piece that he did not have the courage to publish before his "Illumination," namely, *Narcissus, or on the Lover of Himself*. His present prudence replaces his past fear of shame, rooted in the love of himself as loved by others. As shown, as a young man, he thought he had to begin to make a name for himself by a positive contribution to the politicization of philosophy, in its enlightenment component. Now, after his own counter-enlightenment enlightenment, he must put on the same play to render himself "consistent" with his own enlightenment, to achieve full self-knowledge. Again, shame is the obstacle to self-knowledge. To continue, he now knows that the play is a bad play; and that it and he will deserve ridicule, hisses and scorn. Why does he then proceed to render the play public if he already knows and can imagine the outcome? His answer is crucial and is as follows: "I needed (another) test to

19 On the primacy of the political, see G. 101:30n., xi.

achieve full self-knowledge. I did not hesitate to perform it. Once I knew how *my soul* reacted to literary success, it remained for me to see how *it* would react to setbacks. I *now* [after he attended the play he put on, and after its after-party] *know* and can openly state the worst. My play suffered the fate which it deserved and which I had anticipated; but except that it bored me, I left the performance much more satisfied with myself and with better reason (as we will soon see), than if it had succeeded." To foreshadow, he "learned how to live without the esteem of others." He will become true to his nature: "a heart that is too sensitive to other attachments' to be "strongly attached to public opinion" (G. 105:39). Evidently, our mind can deceive us as to the true objects of our soul and visa-versa. Evidently, imaginary deserved scorn is not sufficient to unveil the mystery of the soul. Evidently, we must subject our soul to real experiences in order to discover its true objects.

Moreover, the problem of the gap between Rousseau's "Illumination" or insight and his achievement of "full self-knowledge" is now solved. He passed all the "great tests" of his natural potentials of mind and soul and discovered that he was able to be the naturally good man that he only saw with his mind's eye during his enlightenment. And by publishing *Narcissus, or on the Lover of himself*, he, in one act of philosophical courage, rooted in the love of the truth, in one great prudential deed, he achieved at least three goods. He not only made a "living by the work of his hands," and precluded the audience from worse deeds while ripping them off with a bad play, but also, and more importantly, discovered that he could overcome shame, rooted in his love of himself as loved by others, and hence achieve "full self-knowledge." He can live the life of one who does what is good for him with the least possible harm, or greatest possible good, to others He is a true "lover" and "knower" of the truth. He found his place among men. He now knows among whom he can now "count himself." He can count himself "among the few." The few are clearly identified as those very few, the "exception" that "confirms the rule" of the *First Discourse*, the naturally gifted with the "good fortune" of the combination of "sublime genius" or "celestial intelligence" and a "privileged soul," a strong soul capable of resisting the "current" of the needs of "opinion." He can now count himself as not among the "half philosophers," but among the "genuine" or "true philosophers." He now has a "well-ordered soul," which entails the subordination of recognition to truth, and the love of oneself as loved by others to the love and knowledge of oneself as naturally lovable. He is now as "wise," "good," and "happy" as his nature permits. The only other true or genuine philosopher mentioned is Socrates (twice). Socrates is his new hero and he is his equal. Whereas Augustine venerates God, Rousseau venerates Socrates. Rousseau found his place among men. He is the Socratic of his century: "Only in a very few men of genius does insight into their own ignorance grow as they learn, and they are the only ones for whom study may be good."[20]

Like Augustine, self-knowledge is for Rousseau not without its difficulties. After his achievement of "full self-knowledge" he nevertheless claims that he is under the influence of diametrical opposition, a contradictory self that was not in "principle" resolvable. These are traits of individual, embodied, character or "temperament." They may be inherited. At any rate, they are a consequence of embodied soul and mind. Evidently, since he, just as all human beings, is a natural, complex, contradictory unity of form and matter, of the universal human nature—Rousseau—on the one hand; and of the particular, Jean-Jacques, on the other. He, like all

20 K. 576, 577, 579, 580 G. 110:4, and 92: 1,102:43, 103:35, 104:37, 38, 105:40 17: 38 n., 92:3, 98:20, 102: 33, 83:69. By Socratic of his century I obviously mean Rousseau's understanding of Socrates and of how a Socratic would modify his ways in the context of Rousseau's century. See, L. Sorenson. Rousseau's Socratism: the Political Bearing of "On Theatrical Imitation." Interpretation. 20 (Winter, 1992–1993: 135–155 followed by C. Orwin. Rousseau's Socratism. The Journal of Politics. Vol. 60. No. 1. Feb. 1998: 174–187 and L. Cooper. Emile, or On Philosophy? Rousseau's Modified Platonism. Rousseau and the Ancients and the Moderns. Ed. By Ruth Grant and Phillip Stewart. Montreal: Pensee No. 8. 2001.

humans, is as much the one as the other. As such, he must remain to himself to some extent the object of the "abyss of philosophy," a natural mystery. Moreover, given his "great tests," not God but Rousseau will be the final judge of Jean Jacques.[21]

21 K. 576; See the two ways of knowing "Peter and James" G. 101:30n., 48:55n. See the relation of words to beings G. 147:28–29. See L. Sorenson. "Rousseau's Botanical-Political Problem: On the Nature of Nature and Political Philosophy." A. Ward. From Natural Science to Political Philosophy: Matter and Form. Rowman and Littlefield Press. 2004:195–210. On Rousseau's judgment of himself , see Rousseau Judge of Jean Jacques foreshadowed at K. 580, 574. Compare the beginnings of their Confessions. B. 14–17; K. 5. See also "black bile" or "bilious," K. 572, 574.."

Joyce's Middle Name
Eloise Knowlton

Hugh Kenner begins *A Colder Eye* with a now-famous distinction between facts and "Irish facts." I'd like to begin this essay by eavesdropping on Kenner, "chatting with the pastor of the Church of the Three Patrons, Rathgar":

> I asked him had he known that according to *Ulysses* it was in his church the fictional Leopold Bloom had been baptized prior to espousing the scrupulous Molly, who would countenance many things but not a mixed marriage. He had not; and, one good tidbit deserving another, he confided with husky emphasis, "And do you know who else was baptized in this church? — *James Joyce!*" An Irish Fact. Joyce was not baptized in Three Patrons at all. But he ought to have been, for at least three reasons. (1) He was born nearby. (2) He would surely have been baptized where his Bloom was. (3) Providence in creating the Irish (finest of deeds) endowed them with a craving for occasional emphatic assertions, lacking which the most mellifluous discourse would be but as porter poured upon the floor. It is incumbent on each speaker to furnish these as the structure of discourse prompts, and that which is structurally needful to say, and notably for men of God to say, wise Providence will surely underwrite. (Kenner 3–4)

An Irish fact, then, is a regretfully erroneous statement that feels right, that fits, that "ought to be true," that contributes, in a sportsmanlike manner, to a moment of talk at the needful time, one that wafts the winds of oratory forward, and is not to be too rigorously investigated without putting a drag on the momentum of the tale. A good story bears its truth in the perfection of the telling, and if saying doesn't make it so, well, in the beginning was the Word.

Now, let those made uncomfortable by this lax countenancing of inaccuracy be assured that this paper is built on a fact, a true fact. Joyce's middle name was "Augustine." Or, more strictly speaking still, "Augusta." The name is documented in the most scholarly way in the revised 1982 (which is to say, corrected) Ellmann biography. James Joyce was baptized on 5 February, 1882 at St. Joseph's Chapel of Ease in Roundtown, outside Dublin. The church registry reveals that Joyce's name was entered into the register as "James Augusta Joyce," where, fittingly enough, a gender-inflected graphical error appears at the founding moment of a comic writer who would make much of naming, writing, mistakes, and, in his later works, gender confusion. Most people assume that the name given on that day was in fact "Augustine," and go on with their lives, as Joyce himself seems to have done. He more often used the initial than the name, a gesture that ensured ambiguity. His brother Stanislaus reports that, in addition to his family nickname of "Sunny Jim," one of Joyce's English masters called him "Gussie."

That's a fact. Now for the Irish fact, the "emphatic assertion" needful for this discourse: not only was "Augustine" Joyce's actual middle name, but (speaking metaphorically, and with a casual air) Augustine was his middle name. Augustine's thought, especially as we read it in *Confessions*, pervades and broadly informs Joyce's work, especially *A Portrait of the Artist as a Young Man*.

Like all Irish facts, this grand claim about Joyce's work is (alas) false, but ought to be true. Consider how much the two had in common: both were highly intelligent, highly ambitious young men, who came of age at the edges of dying empires. As young boys, both were left to their own devices between schools, when their fathers couldn't pay the fees. Both were bookish, in passionate conversation with their reading, and both were ferociously committed and prolific writers. Both enjoyed academic disquisition, and were happy to mix it up in contention and debate. Both were intensely aware of and keenly interested in the weight of the past, personal and public. They were prodigal sons, careerists, sinners, wanderers. They were blessed with devoted and devout mothers they ran from, but couldn't escape. They were equipped with good Latin and no Greek. Both were fundamentally concerned with the spiritual investigation of the self, with belief, sin and redemption, with the strength and legitimacy of the Church, and with the urgencies of conscience. Both revolutionized writing about the self, one by all-but inventing autobiography, the other by forever transforming it. It feels right to say that Joyce, the latter-day Catholic, found Augustine, the early Church father, a powerful influence. What matter if the earlier figure contributed to the building and strengthening of the Church, and the latter to its rejection or reformation? Even that opposition is a satisfyingly exact one.

Further, and working now from Augustine to Joyce, Peter Brown describes in his chapter on *Confessions* a book that sounds, to a Joycean, strangely familiar. Brown reminds us that, in its time, *Confessions* was a "startling" book in which "traditional forms of literary expression...would be transformed beyond recognition." (Brown 158 passim) Brown reminds us that *Confessions* is, "an exceptionally difficult book," and that Augustine "paid his audience the great compliment as if they were as steeped in Platonic philosophy as himself." Brown calls the *Confessions,* "a manifesto of the inner world," and finally, and perhaps most importantly, Brown tells us that "Augustine analyses his past feelings with ferocious honesty. They were too important to him to be falsified by sentimental stereotypes."

Augustine influenced Joyce. It ought to be true, and on a grand scale, factually. What factual evidence do we have for this? Joyce read Augustine. It's evident from the works that he did so. Augustine appears by name or by identifiable language in nearly all of them. He's quoted in a very early Joyce essay, "Drama and Life." (Ellmann 70–3) He puts in at least two appearances in *Portrait*, and two in *Ulysses*, and is scattered liberally over *Finnegan's Wake*, where he appears as "Ecclectiastes of Hippo" (38.29) and

"Angustissimost" (104.6), and where James Atherton finds his "felix culpa" rendered as, "O Phoenix Culprit!"

Any consideration of Joyce's influences should immediately acknowledge that Joyce had a lot of them. He read everything, high low and in between, *Confessions* and *Genesis* right alongside *The Irish Homestead* and *Tit Bits*, and that motley textuality floods his works in a great tide, rising as Joyce's work matured, and bursting past all reasonable dikes in *Finnegans Wake*. This is part of what has kept the professors busy for, so far, nearly one hundred of the three hundred years Joyce predicted. What we experience when we read Joyce is his creative transformation of lived experience, but also and increasingly as his work developed, his creative transformation of received textuality, and in this he and the Augustine of the *Confessions* are very much alike. Both live very much, and very critically, in the archive. Of course, as Harold Bloom would point out, this tension with the writers of the past brings with it companion anxieties about authorial precedence, power, and origin, and indeed, in one of his late self-portraits in *Finnegans Wake*, Joyce calls himself uneasily, a "Pelagiarist" and a "scissors and paste man." Joyce's relationship to the tradition was close, but uncomfortable.

It is a fact, then, that Joyce read Augustine. What happened then? I'd like to look closely at three (factual) appearances of Augustine in Joyce's work, sightings which may help us peer into the question of what Joyce did with (or perhaps, to) Augustine. Then, I'd like to return to my Irish fact, and discuss the broader effect *Confessions* should have had on Joyce's work, particularly *A Portrait of the Artist as a Young Man*.

Drama and Life

Augustine's first appearance in Joyce's work is in "Drama and Life," an essay Joyce read at the age of 18 to the Literary and Historical Society of University College, Dublin, early in 1900. Joyce had fallen under the chilly spell of realist dramatist Henrik Ibsen, little known in Ireland at the time, but for Joyce a bracing model for putting real life, meaning ordinary, unromanticized, unexpurgated, banal, middle-class, life, on the stage, and Joyce's somewhat bombastic essay is infused with the desire to reject the phonies and tell it like it is. For Joyce, drama — real drama — wasn't meant to be edifying or uplifting. Drama wasn't, as another Irishman associated with play put it, "The good end happily and the bad unhappily." For this very young Joyce, drama, with all aesthetic work, soared above any pedagogical burden, and for this reason the president of UCD, having read Joyce's essay in his role as censor, objected to it on the grounds of Joyce's indifference to ethical purpose. He asked for some changes, or he wouldn't permit it to be read. In a tense meeting, related in embellished form in *Stephen* Hero and *A Portrait*, Joyce refused, and ultimately (by way of Aquinas) convinced him to permit the essay to stand as written.

Joyce read the paper on the evening of January 20 in what must have been a fairly hostile environment, both from college authorities and from his fellow students, who had, just the week before, cheered an essay praising Greek drama's enduring power. Ellmann suggests that some of the more orthodox students may have been coached to attack Joyce in the question and answer session that followed the paper. (Ellmann 71)

Joyce had come to spread the word that Greek drama, all right enough in its time, had long since ossified into a pack of meaningless conventions, interesting only to historians, and observed only by the hidebound and the fearful. Joyce proclaims

> Drama will be for the future at war with convention, if it is to realize itself truly.... Drama of so wholehearted and admirable a nature cannot but draw all hearts from the spectacular and the theatrical, its note being truth and freedom in every aspect of it. It may be asked — what are we to do — in the words of Tolstoi. First, clear our minds of cant and alter the falsehoods to which we have lent our support. Let us criticize in the manner of free people, as a free race, recking little of ferula and formula.... *Securus judicat orbis terrarum*, is not too high a motto for all human artwork.

Securus judicat orbis terrarum: "Untroubled, the world judges." That's Augustine, from *Contra Epistolam Parmeniani,* III, 24. Lifted not directly from that work, as Ellmann reminds us, but via Cardinal Henry Newman's *Apologia Pro Vita Sua.* In this moment, and with this audience, Joyce can give it, untranslated, to an audience he knows will recognize it, and will recognize with it the nimbus of Newman, who, by the way, founded UCD. He can know that it will carry weight, a father of the church invoked from within the words of the founder of the college at which he speaks. Faced with the hostile authorities of church and school, Joyce invokes a higher authority, Augustine and Newman support his claim of truth above all else: a rhetor's use of a rhetor's words. "Untroubled, the world judges," as a motto for art and the artist will later find expression in other Joycean phrases: "The artist is away, paring his fingernails..." and "The great refrigerating apparatus."

James Atherton reminds us that William York Tindall reminded him that the quote in the original Augustine, discussing the fate of exiles, speaks against just this kind of isolation. "The calm judgment of the world is that those men cannot be good who in any part of the world cut themselves off from the rest of the world," (Atherton 141, Tindall 11), but Joyce didn't get that part in the Newman. What do these facts tell us? That Joyce was very young. That he had learned to use authority against authority, and that he wasn't above taking what he needed and twisting it to his own ends. His use of Augustine here is, well, you guessed it, an Irish fact: an emphatic statement no less impressive and necessary for all infidelity to its origin, a truth in itself. It ought to be true. But at this point, Augustine is, for Joyce, no more than a voice heard off, a rhetorical weapon apprehended secondhand, a name, not a middle name.

Aeolus, God of the Winds

Leaping over *Dubliners,* where he is not named, and *A Portrait,* where he is adduced twice in the most unpleasant light, Augustine appears next in the midst of Joyce's mature work, in the "Aeolus" chapter of *Ulysses.* We aren't surprised to find Augustine the Rhetorician showing up here, this being the episode devoted to things windy and oratorical, a chapter full of windbags and blowhards. Its organ is, of course, the lung. Stephen has come to the offices of the *Freeman's Journal* to get his boss's prolix letter on hoof and mouth disease — Joyce chose his ailment carefully — printed. When Stephen arrives, the topic under discussion in the newsroom is Great Speeches of the Past, and Prof. MacHugh declaims from memory an actual (factual, not Irish factual) speech given October 24, 1901 by John F. Taylor, advocating the return of the Irish language in Ireland. The words are stirring, and Stephen is stirred. MacHugh

> ...raised his head firmly. His eyes bethought themselves once more. Witless shellfish swam in the gross lenses to and fro seeking outlet. He began: *Mr. chairman, ladies and gentlemen: Great was my admiration in listening to the remarks addressed to the youth of Ireland a moment since by my learned friend. It seemed to me that I had been transported into a country away from this country, into an age remote from this age, that I stood in ancient Egypt and that I was listening to the speech of some highpriest of that land addressed to the youthful Moses.* His listeners held their cigarettes poised to hear, their smokes ascending in frail stalks that flowered with his speech. *And let our crooked smokes.* Noble words coming. Look out. Could you try your hand at it yourself? *— And it seemed to me that I heard the voice of that Egyptian highpriest raised in a tone of like haughtiness and like pride. I heard his words, and their meaning was revealed to me.* (U 116–17)

Joyce has MacHugh recite a speech that begins with a laudatory appraisal of a previous speech in which he, Taylor, confesses to being "transported," Chinese boxes of powerful quotation opening one inside the other. We know Stephen is highly susceptible to the sound and meaning of words and has been since a boy ("Pull out his eyes/ Apologise,") and the grown Stephen, warier now, knows he is susceptible: "Look out." But his wariness isn't enough to fend off what happens next: the unexpected and unpreventable appearance of Augustine.

"FROM THE FATHERS," centered on the page and in all caps, bumps into the text, and as swiftly disappears — one of Aeolus's famous headlines — and we are back in Stephen's mind, expecting to see his response to MacHugh's recitation of Taylor's words. But what comes into Stephen's mind, triggered by Taylor's "It was revealed to me," is, instead: "It was revealed to me that, those things are good which yet are corrupted, which neither if they were supremely good, nor unless they are good, could be corrupted." Stephen adds, "Ah, curse you! That's saint Augustine." (Joyce, *Ulysses* 117)

It is indeed, from Book VII of the *Confessions*, a passage that marks the culmination of a long and painful search for the origins of evil in a good creation. Augustine considers and discards one explanation after another, until he turns inward to listen to God's. Here is the passage from the less impacted 1991 Chadwick translation:

> It was obvious to me that things which are liable to corruption are good. If they were supreme goods, or if they were not good at all, they could not be corrupted. For if they were supreme goods, they would be incorruptible. If there were no good in them, there would be nothing capable of being corrupted. (Augustine VII xii, 18)

Nothing could be more logical, reason pointing plainly to a truth of faith. And nothing could be more affirming of the flawed life of the everyday, the banality of evil in which Stephen finds himself, and which all his works so ruthlessly show.

While Joyce clearly made USE of Augustine in "Drama and Life," marshalling him to the service of his view of art, in *Ulysses* Augustine appears unbidden in Stephen's mind and has his say. In the profane environment of workaday Dublin, a gleam of Augustine appears, and an Augustine who comes precisely affirming the goodness of a corrupted world. Stephen's disgusted recognition, "Ah, curse you, that's saint Augustine," registers Stephen's conflicted state: in full retreat from a literary and religious tradition that is nevertheless deeply part of him. Jean Kimball has (brilliantly) suggested that while Stephen is associated with the intellect and Aquinas, Bloom is more associated with Augustine and love, and indeed, she has convincingly argued for Augustine as the proximate influence in the "love loves" passage of the "Cyclops" episode. (Kimball 376) Here, Stephen cannot shut Augustine out. He can only recognize and reject him.

This appearance reveals more than simply Joyce's interest in the workings of Stephen's mind, and the power of his reading (Augustine among many) on his moment-to-moment consciousness. It is by now a critical nostrum that Joyce's mature work turns to a broad affirmation of life, an embracing of the world as a flawed but nevertheless good place. *Ulysses*, like *The Odyssey,* is comic, in that first sense of comedy, as an affirmation of life, over and against the tragic vision of *The Iliad*. It is through Augustine, and precisely the Augustine of this passage, that Joyce would have seen this affirmation articulated within his philosophic and theological tradition: a significant sighting.

"Aeolus" concludes with the anti-rhetoric of Stephen's "Parable of the Plums," a lean and hungry answer to the rhetorical *sirocco* blowing. "Plums" eschews all ornament and unwinds in the manner (perhaps a little too much in the manner) of *Dubliners*: stark plainstyle, inconclusive, documentary, excessively detailed, realist and, viewed in hindsight, obscene. The mature Joyce depicts himself finding a voice in as un-allusive and non-literary a style as you could ask for. It's a question of control. If Stephen can't control the voices of the past, if *Confessions* (and a hundred other texts) will intrude, he will hew to a style that sheds all trace of tradition:

Two Dublin vestals have lived fifty and fiftythree years
in Fumbally's alley. They want to see the views of Dublin

from the top of Nelson's Pillar. They save up three and tenpence in a red tin letterbox moneybox. They shake out the threepenny bits and sixpences and coax out the pennies with the blade of a knife. Two and three in silver and one and seven in coppers. They put on their bonnets and best clothes and take their umbrellas for fear it may come on to rain. (U 119–20)

"They shake out the threepenny bits and sixpences and coax out the pennies with the blade of a knife." That's the true scrupulous meanness of a *Dubliners* tale, could almost serve as a gloss on Yeats's "September 1913": "What need you, being come to sense,/But fumble in a greasy till/And add the halfpence to the pence/And prayer to shivering prayer, until/You have dried the marrow from the bone?" Romantic Ireland is dead and gone, Yeats says in 1914. And a good thing, too, Joyce replies in 1922.

Finnegans Wake

So far, we have seen Augustine 1. deployed (with strong intent) as a weapon, and 2. appearing (unbidden and unwelcome) as a revelation. Joyce's last book shows Augustine again, heavily draped in the Wake Treatment, but still recognizable. James Atherton, in his *The Books at the Wake*, spots *Confessions* at 223.39 and 422.10, and perhaps later in the fable of the Ondt and the Gracehoper. As sample, let's take the earlier passage. Augustine writes in Book X:

> And what is the object of my love? I asked the earth and it answered: "It is not I." I asked all that is in it; they made the same confession (Job28:12f). I asked the sea, the deeps, the living creatures that creep, and they responded: 'We are not your God, look beyond us.' I asked the breezes which blow and the entire air with its inhabitants said: Anaximenes was mistaken; I am not God. I asked heaven, sun, moon and stars; they said: 'Nor are

we the God whom you seek.' And I said to all these things in my external environment: 'Tell me of my God who you are not, tell me something about him." And with a great voice they cried out: "He made us." (Ps.99:3). My question was the attention I gave to them, and their response was their beauty. (*Confessions* X)

A beautiful passage, redolent of that restlessness we associate essentially with Augustine. It appears in *Finnegans Wake* in Book Two, section one, "The Children's Hour," where the children are at play in a question and answer game Joyce identified as "Angels and Devils," that serves as the schema for the chapter. Reminiscent of the "Eumaius" chapter of *Ulysses*, Joyce thought this chapter the happiest of book (Eckley 130). In the night-language of the *Wake,* the rational thought of daytime undergoes a strange transmogrification:

He askit of the hoothed fireshield but it was undergone into the matthued heaven. He soughed it from the luft but that bore ne mark ne message. He luked upon the bloomingrund where ongly his corns were growning. At last he listed bach to beckline how she pranked alone so johntily. (FW 223.39)

Joyce may have been drawn initially to Augustine by the association of children's games. Famously, Augustine's moment of conversion begins with what might be children at play. He recounts hearing

...chanting as if it might be a boy or a girl (I do not know which), saying and repeating over and over again 'Pick up and read, pick up and read.' At once my countenance changed, and I began to think intently whether there might be some sort of children's game in which such a chant is used. But I could not remember having heard of one. (*Confessions*, VIII.xi.29)

Joyce may have been drawn more particularly to this passage by its use of the four Aristotelian elements: earth, air, fire, and water, found throughout the *Wake,* along with other structures of four: seasons and squares, as well as the four books of the *Wake* itself: the Books of the Parents, the Book of the Sons, the Book of the People, and the Recorso, or Return. Here, the four elements are joined with the names of the four gospellers, each clothed in a different part of speech: "matthued," (adjective); "mark," (noun) "luked," (verb); and "johntily" (adverb).

So deeply imbedded as to be almost invisible, *Confessions* guides the *Wake* passage without attribution, an invisible force, a fully assimilated voice. Here at the end of all Joyce, Augustine becomes one of the myriad voices the all-but blind Joyce claimed were writing *Finnegans Wake.* (Ellmann 6) No longer Augustine's master, as in "Drama and Life," nor his resistant rememberer, as in "Aeolus," the Joyce of *Finnegans Wake* has ceded control and allows Augustine to speak through him, a guiding spirit rather than an identifiable scholarly source.

Confessions and *Portrait*

Factually, we've found Augustine in Joyce's works early and late, and now we come to where our Irish Facticity would most expect him to be seen: *A Portrait of the Artist as a Young Man.* How could a writer such as Joyce, having read *Confessions,* write a strongly autobiographical work about his spiritual coming into being, without being strongly influenced by Augustine's spiritual autobiography? As if to discourage any such speculation, the Joyce of *Portrait* has sent Augustine to hell, as it were: in his only two appearances, he's associated with damnation. First, he is invoked in one of the terrifying retreat sermons, ("...moreover, as saint Augustine points out, God will impart to them [the damned souls in hell] His own knowledge of sin so that sin will appear to them in all its hideous malice as it appears to the eyes of God Himself"). Then, he is adduced among Stephen's friends as demonstrative of the cruelty of the Roman Catholic Church (" — Saint Augustine says that about unbaptised children going to hell, Temple answered, because he was a cruel old sinner too.") (*Portrait* 132, 240)

Confessions and *Portrait*: both interrogate their pasts with uncompromising honesty. Both get to truth through the immediate, the experiential, the lived, the particular, even the banal. Both constitute mighty projects of suffering and struggle that lead to affirmations of vocation and spiritual commitment. I'd like to conclude this essay with the claim (Irish fact) that what Joyce gained from *Confessions*, particularly for *Portrait*, was not a model of style, or of form, or of will to honesty, but something quite specific to the Augustine of *Confessions*: autobiography as an act of becoming, as a kind of performative.

In 1955, J.L. Austin travelled from Oxford to Harvard to give the William James Lectures. He began by distinguishing ordinary language, language that describes, which he called "constative" language, from language that acts, that performs which, he called "performative": "I do," in vowing; "I name," in christening; "I give and bequeath," in willing; "I bet you sixpence," in wagering. (Austin 5) Austin argues that this kind of utterance is peculiar in that it DOES something rather than SAYS something: it puts pressure on the notion of language as exclusively representative or communicative. Now, while no one would argue that either *Confessions* or *Portrait* consists of performative statements, taken as a whole — even as the sacrament of confession can be taken — they constitute actions, as much as statements. They DO something, rather than simply SAY something, and things are different —for their authors, and for their readers — after they have occurred. In both, moments are recalled from memory, and put under a kind of moral microscope, more overtly in *Confessions*, as the form permits, more indirectly in the novel, as Joyce refined his work from an initial 1904 sketch, through a longer manuscript (*Stephen Hero*), into the leaner, modernistically-inflected novel of 1914. Both governing voices have searched their pasts long and hard, and both have found their truth within.

This, from *Confessions*:

See how widely I have ranged, Lord, searching for you in my memory. I have not found you outside it. For I have found nothing coming from you which I have not stored in my memory since the time I first learnt of you. Since the day I learnt of you, I have never forgotten you. Where I discovered the truth there I found my God, truth itself, which from the time I learnt it, I have not forgotten. And so, since the time I learnt of you, you remain in my consciousness, and there I find you when I recall you and delight in you. (*Confessions* X.xxiii.35)

By looking inward, Augustine found God, truth, and himself. His confession enacts a revelatory reconciliation between himself as a creation of God, and by this act does he comes into being as himself. The fact that a great deal of church doctrine also comes into being is an extra bonus.

In the same way, Joyce shows Stephen experiencing the sins of Augustine: sins in their full range, sensual and spiritual. But confession, for Joyce, must be stripped of its association with the Church, where it is represented as degrading, before this inward turning can be spiritually transformative. Stephen's fear-induced confession, made at 16, after the retreat, avails him nothing, and is marked as more a bodily riddance than a spiritual cleansing:

His sins trickled from his lips, one by one, trickled in shameful drops from his soul festering and oozing like a sore, a squalid stream of vice. The last sins oozed forth, sluggish, filthy. There was no more to tell. He bowed his head, overcome. (148)

Yet Stephen will have his Augustinian moment of revelation, and it will be couched as a return from the unknowing, deathlike past. In the bird-girl revelation on the beach, Stephen's

...soul had arisen from the grave of boyhood, spurning her graveclothes. Yes! Yes! Yes! He would create proudly out of the freedom and power of his soul, as the great artificer whose name he bore, a living thing, new and soaring and beautiful, impalpable, imperishable. (*Portrait* 174)

A new spiritual creation is born, or re-born, and will create out of himself new ways of writing, new ways of thinking about human experience, even, in the end, a new language. The artificer whose "name Stephen bore," is, of course, Daedalus. The artificer whose name Joyce bore, was Augustine.

At the Still Point: T.S. Eliot's *Confessions*
Glenn C. Arbery

No poet in the English language has written more philosophically about time and history than T.S. Eliot in his *Four Quartets*, the series of poems published from 1936 to 1942. It is no surprise that the poems have elicited comparisons to St. Augustine's *Confessions*, especially to Books X and XI. Only recently has commentary begun to turn to a different dimension of *Four Quartets* that can also be fruitfully explored in Augustinian terms—that is, the autobiographical presence of Eliot in these poems. In *Four Quartets*, as William Melaney points out, "Eliot explores his poetic development as an autobiographical concern that challenges the way that his work has been persistently read in modern criticism."[1] Eliot, of course, contributed mightily to the way he has been "persistently read" by emphasizing in "Tradition and the Individual Talent" that poetry is not the expression of personality, but "an escape from personality."[2] But the *Four Quartets* clearly differ from earlier poems such as "The Love Song of J. Alfred Prufrock," *The Waste Land*, or "Ash Wednesday." Eliot's use of four locations with special personal meaning for him—Burnt Norton in Gloucestershire, East Coker in Somerset, the Dry Salvages off the coast of Massachusetts, and Little Gidding in

---

1   See William D. Melaney, "T. S. Eliot's Poetics of Self: Reopening 'Four Quartets.'" *Alif: Journal of Comparative Poetics.* No. 22, (2002), pp. 148–168. Stable URL: http://www.jstor.org/stable/1350054.
2   T.S. Eliot, "Tradition and the Individual Talent." *The Sacred Wood.* New York: Alfred A. Knopf, 1921; Bartleby.com, 1996. www.bartleby.com/200/sw4.html#3.

Cambridgeshire—strongly suggests the autobiographical context, and for all their philosophical abstraction, the poems are unexpectedly "confessional," though obviously not in the mode of Robert Lowell or Sylvia Plath. Like Augustine, Eliot finds in his own experience the providential pattern that informs that weds history to the timeless Word.

Eliot does not cite the *Confessions* in justifying his mode of reserved personal reference (as Dante felt it necessary to do in the *Convivio*), but his meditations on the "timeless moments" that constitute history, including his own history, have their parallels in Augustine's narration of key points in his life. They illustrate what Eliot calls the "intersection of the timeless/With time."[3] Like the *Confessions* or the *Divine Comedy*, the poems use personal experience as the necessary and unavoidable basis of their theological and philosophical meditations. Eliot pares his biography back to essential metonymies—places and things associated with key moments, either of his own life or the lives of others that he has made his own. He leaves out details—more even than Augustine—and in a sense, this reticence seems odd. Eliot himself writes that "What poetry proves about any philosophy is merely its possibility for being lived... For poetry... is not the assertion that something is true, but the making that truth more fully real to us; it is the creation of a sensuous embodiment. It is the making the Word Flesh."[4] Yet if he himself is "proving a philosophy," then in these poems he is doing so more on the level of argument or perhaps of deeply felt ideas than of the sensuously embodied experience of poetry. The movement of the whole series never presents an imaginatively inhabitable bodily image of Eliot like the one Dante repeatedly presents of himself in the *Divine Comedy* (weighing down Phlegyas'

---

3   T.S. Eliot, *Four Quartets*. Orlando: Harvest Books, 1971, p. 44. All parenthetical citations of the poems will refer to the page numbers of this edition.

4   Cited in Martin Warner, "Philosophical Poetry: The Case of Four Quartets," *Philosophy and Literature*, Volume 10, Number 2, October 1986, p. 225.

boat, for example, or casting a shadow on Mt. Purgatory). He never dramatizes his struggle with an idea in the way Dostoyevsky does with Raskolnikov in *Crime and Punishment* by showing through Raskolnikov the idea of necessary transgression precisely in "its possibility for being lived." So spare is Eliot's self-presentation that it has been difficult even to see its contours as autobiography. Yet the pattern is clearly there from his earliest childhood in St. Louis to the historical uncertainty of World War II; the poems even anticipate his eventual burial in the church in East Coker. Poverty of detail nevertheless yields density of symbol. The *Four Quartets* as a whole can be considered Eliot's twentieth century refiguring of the *Confessions* as philosophical poetry, a vein as far as possible from the revelation of former sensual transgressions that most moderns (like most of Augustine's contemporaries) would very much prefer.

1

Eliot's engagement with St. Augustine was already of long standing when he came to *Four Quartets*. One famous reference occurs at the end of "The Fire Sermon," the third section of *The Waste Land* (1922) that includes the tryst between "the young man carbuncular" and the "typist home at teatime":

To Carthage then I came

Burning burning burning burning
O Lord Thou pluckest me out
O Lord Thou pluckest

burning (307–11)

No reader would necessarily think of Augustine in the reference to Carthage. Those alert to the *Aeneid* allusions earlier in the poem would be more likely to remember the far more famous arrival of Aeneas in the city that Rome would eventually destroy, but Eliot underscores his debt to St. Augustine in his notes, where the sequence of references is illuminating:

307. V. St. Augustine's *Confessions*: "to Carthage then I came, where a cauldron of unholy loves sang all about mine ears."

308. The complete text of the Buddha's Fire Sermon (which corresponds in importance to the Sermon on the Mount) from which these words are taken, will be found translated in the late Henry Clarke Warren's Buddhism in Translation (Harvard Oriental Series). Mr. Warren was one of the great pioneers of Buddhist studies in the occident.

309. From St. Augustine's Confessions again. The collocation of these two representatives of eastern and western asceticism, as the culmination of this part of the poem, is not an accident.[5]

Eliot not only includes his explicit allusions to Buddha's Fire Sermon and the *Confessions* in these lines, but he also layers the story of Augustine's conversion onto the story of Aeneas. Jupiter "plucks" Aeneas away from Carthage, Dido kills herself, and Aeneas sails toward Italy with her pyre burning ominously behind him. Eliot might also have in mind the Roman destruction of Carthage in 146 BC, because the lines would fit: "To Carthage then I came/burning burning burning burning." Twenty years before the conclusion of the *Four Quartets*, Eliot's understanding of tradition made possible this poetic juxtaposition of images and allusions. He already had a vivid sense of the co-presence of the whole tradition, eastern and western, of which Augustine forms a crucial part. In "Tradition and the Individual Talent," he writes that tradition "cannot be inherited, and if you want it you must obtain it by great labor. It involves, in the first place, the historical sense ... a

---

5   Eliot makes Augustine the western parallel to Buddha, but his asceticism might not be the first thing that comes to mind for most readers; a more likely candidate, in fact, might be St. Anthony of Egypt, whose biography Augustine himself mentions in Book VIII of the *Confessions*.

perception, not only of the pastness of the past, but of its presence." Any author who possesses the historical sense, he said, will write "with a feeling that the whole of the literature of Europe from Homer and within it the whole of the literature of his own country has a simultaneous existence and composes a simultaneous order." Moreover, he went on to argue, "when a new work of art is created, something happens simultaneously to all the works of art which preceded it."[6]

Scholars now discern many autobiographical elements in *The Waste Land*, such as the dialogue between the married couple in Section II, "A Game of Chess," which echoes the strained conversations between Eliot and his wife Vivienne. But, unlike the *Four Quartets*, the earlier poem carefully suppresses overtly traceable personal references in favor of cultural ones. With the historical sense comes a new awareness of time. History is revealed not as a succession of events and causes but as an accumulation of moments; these cultural memory traces are not necessarily ordered sequentially, but—at least in the poetic practice of *The Waste Land*—clustered by associations, like the contents of the unconscious. History is a memory acquired only after the "great labor" of obtaining the tradition, but, once acquired, its means of access becomes one's own act of ordering recollection. Far from being an unearned legacy into which one happens by being born in a certain time and place, the tradition is an earned, dynamic, and changing unity like the one discovered by the reader who would master *The Waste Land*. Reading the poem is analogous to what Augustine describes in searching one's memory: "The huge repository of the memory, with its secret and unimaginable caverns, welcomes and keeps all these things, to be reached and brought out for use when needed."[7] History in this sense does indeed mean the presence of the past, because the historical past not only becomes part of

6   "Tradition and the Individual Talent," 3. Accessed March 9, 2012.
7   *The Confessions*, trans. Maria Boulding, O.S.A. (New York: New City Press, 2010), p. 188. All subsequent citations will be from this text.

individual experience (since the act of recollection is obviously an internal phenomenon), but in becoming part of it gathers it into greater than personal significance.[8]

Louis Dupre observes that ""Memory never copies the past: it constitutes it as past by breathing new life into a bygone reality, and by placing it in a wholly new context. Thus memory mysteriously revives the past in a new time and a new space."[9] When Eliot revives the line from the *Confessions*, which already formed part of his own memory, Augustine's personal memory—"To Carthage then I came"—becomes part of Eliot's poem. Eliot's historical associations are overlaid on those that Augustine demonstrably brought to Carthage, since the *Aeneid* plays an important part in Book I of the *Confessions*. The reader, in turn, brings his own associations, including (perhaps) the moment of first encountering Eliot's line and the note about it in a particular time and place. That moment, recollected later as the first prompting, it may be, of an interest in Augustine's story of conversion, becomes timeless as well; its significance has little to do with the succession of events in the ordinary time surrounding it and more to do with a pattern of similar moments. Eliot writes in "The Dry Salvages," the third

8   Knowledge of history, on the other hand, does not guarantee access to the truth, as the speaker of Eliot's "Gerontion" (1920) complains:

>Think now
>History has many cunning passages, contrived corridors
>And issues, deceives with whispering ambitions,
>Guides us by vanities. Think now
>She gives when our attention is distracted
>And what she gives, gives with such supple confusions
>That the giving famishes the craving

   Poems. From New York: A.A. Knopf, 1920; Bartleby.com, 2011. www.bartleby.com/199.html#33–39. Accessed March 10, 2012.

9   Louis Dupré, "Alienation and Redemption through Time and Memory: An Essay on Religious Time Consciousness," *Journal of the American Academy of Religion*, Vol. 43, No. 4 (December 1975), p. 673.

poem in *Four Quartets*, "It seems, as one becomes older,/That the past has another pattern, and ceases to be a mere sequence" (39). In other words, events in the past take on their importance only in the memory: "We had the experience but missed the meaning,/And approach to the meaning restores the experience/In a different form" (39). Moreover, "the past experience revived in the mean-ing/Is not the experience of one life only/But of many generations" (39).

2

In the past twenty-five years, biographers have done perhaps too good a job in exploring areas of Eliot's "one life only" once closed to public view. In particular, Lyndall Gordon's investigations of Eliot's relations with Emily Hale, the American woman he might have married instead of Vivienne Haigh-Wood, have been so ex-planatory as to be reductive, and criticism of the poem must now avoid the same biographical trap from which Eliot and the New Critics wanted to free poetry early in the 20th century. Nevertheless, by naming the first poem "Burnt Norton," Eliot himself invites the question of the place's meaning to him, and Gordon provides a con-vincing answer by showing that he visited Burnt Norton with Emily Hale in 1934.[10] Given the biographical context, Eliot's lines about "the passage which we did not take/Towards the door we never opened/Into the rose-garden" take on an intensely personal mean-ing. To be sure, the meaning has always been the subjunctive possi-bility—Frost's "road not taken." On the other hand, it does not hurt to recognize Emily Hale. At the center of this almost forbiddingly abstract poem is Eliot's personal meditation on the possibility of a different and happier life of fulfillment. The "rose-garden" seems a natural symbol of it. "The hidden laughter/Of children in the fo-liage" might name a possibility "Only in a world of speculation," but it is a deeply felt possibility nonetheless.

10 See Lyndall Gordon, *T.S. Eliot: An Imperfect Life*. New York: Nor-ton, 1999.

To rescue Eliot from reductively biographical considerations, it is only necessary to remember the context of St. Augustine and Dante. What happens in an individual life, given a kind of attentive openness to Providence and a bold sense of the seriousness of one's own experience, takes on universal significance once symbolic importance emerges in a pattern. Dante's first sight of Beatrice at the age of nine, for example, comes to stand for an epiphany, almost a theophany, whose importance emerges only by the end of the *Divine Comedy*. Similarly, Augustine's theft of pears from a pear tree when he was a boy takes on dense symbolic importance because of its resonance with the original theft in Eden and other passages (such as the recognition of Nathaniel under the fig tree in John 1:48) in his enlarged and biblically informed memory. Eliot's awareness of the tradition means that his personal experience can be taken up and transfigured by finding a larger pattern of those "timeless moments" that truly elicit meditations on their significance.

The four poems of the *Quartets*, which can be analyzed in terms of their elemental associations (air, earth, water, and fire respectively), can also be understood to constitute a symbolically complete biographical meditation. Like the *Confessions*, which centers on a number of significant places in Augustine's life—Tagaste, Carthage, Rome, Milan, and Ostia come to mind—the poems center on places of what Eliot calls "the life of significant soil," including the ones "where prayer has been valid." "Burnt Norton" considers Eliot's unhappy marriage, not directly, but in terms of a symbolically realized alternative available to his imagination; "East Coker" examines his genealogical rootedness in England, since this village is the one from which Eliot's remote ancestor set out to come to America; "The Dry Salvages" recalls Eliot's American early life on the Mississippi River in St. Louis and on the coast of Massachusetts; and" Little Gidding," set in the village where a robustly spiritual Anglican community once thrived under Nicholas Ferrar and where Charles I visited after his defeat by Cromwell's forces, draws upon Eliot's powerful, elective identification with royalism and Anglo-Catholicism, not to mention with the history of England. As Joseph Schwartz has put it, "These places, treated in serial fashion and with growing intensity, are the means by which memory is awakened and the imagination, aroused by the concrete, is made free. They are personal places where history happens for the modern orphaned speaker of the poem."[11]

Eliot emphasizes that what he is doing in these poems—indeed, in his career as a whole— is a kind of repetition. As he writes in "East Coker,"

> what there is to discover
> By strength and submission, has already been discovered
> Once or twice, or several times, by men whom one cannot hope
> To emulate—but there is no competition—
> There is only the fight to recover what has been lost
> nd found and lost again and again: and now, under conditions
> That seem unpropitious.

In Section II of "Little Gidding," this work of recovery is put a little differently by the shade that the speaker meets on a London street after an air raid. This recently dead poet (a composite dominated by W. B. Yeats), says that "last year's words belong to last year's language/And next year's words await another voice." The truer sense of time might be centuries or epochs. What Augustine did in his day (or what Dante did 900 years later) needs to be done again in Eliot's, in his own language, in part "To purify the dialect of the tribe/And urge the mind to aftersight and foresight."

In *Four Quartets*, time per se moves to the center of Eliot's concern, because of its intensely personal—that is, intensely *felt*—importance. He begins "Burnt Norton," the first poem of the sequence, on an abstract, meditative note:

Time present and time past
Are both perhaps present in time future,
And time future contained in time past.
If all time is eternally present
All time is unredeemable.

---

11 Joseph Schwartz, "The Theology of History in T.S. Eliot's *Four Quartets*," *Logos: A Journal of Catholic Thought and Culture*, Volume 2, Number 1, Winter 1999, 35–36.

St. Paul writes in Ephesians 5: "See then that ye walk circum-spectly, not as fools, but as wise,/Redeeming the time, because the days are evil." The opening of "Burnt Norton" seems to be a direct response to Paul's injunction. Like Augustine in Book XI of the *Confessions*, Eliot's speaker takes up the three tenses of time and then imagines all time gathered into eternal presence. To whom could it be eternally present if not to God? But "If all time is eter-nally present/All time is unredeemable," he writes. St. Paul enjoins Christians to redeem the time, but how can time be redeemed if it is always already complete—a fixed and determined structure that cannot be anything other than what it is? All time, in that case, would have the unchangeable quality of the past.

Nietzsche's Zarathustra says that "the will, the emancipator" becomes a torturer and takes revenge on everything "because it cannot go backward"—that is, because it cannot change the fixed past. Dido, for example, cannot change the fact that Aeneas aban-doned her because of his divine call to found Rome. But she *can* will for her people to take revenge on Rome in the future. "This alone is revenge itself," writes Nietzsche, "the will's antipathy to-wards time, and time's '*It was*.'"[12] In other words, revenge arises from the powerlessness of the will to change the past, and revenge is a far cry from redemption. In Genesis, Joseph might have taken revenge on his brothers for selling him to the Ishmaelites, for ex-ample, but instead, he redeems their bad action when, through God's providence, he becomes the agent of their redemption. Eliot could use his poetry to take revenge on Vivienne Haigh-Wood for making his life a torment, but instead he pursues a different route, recognizing, perhaps, both in what she made possible for him as the voice of his age, and also in the meditation Emily Hale prompts on an alternative realized only in the imagination, a providential design. Eliot finds a way toward redemption precisely in the un-folding experience of time, in his dramatically realized relation to history, which thus includes both what happens and what might

12 Friedrich Nietzsche, *Thus Spoke Zarathustra*. Trans. R. J. Hollingdale (New York: Penguin Books, 1969), 162.

have happened. Near the end of the last poem of the sequence, "Little Gidding," he writes, "A people without history/Is not redeemed from time, for history is a pattern/Of timeless moments" (58).

3

But what characterizes "timeless moments" and what exactly constitutes a "pattern"? Eliot's allusions, such as the Carthage reference in *The Waste Land*, might provide a clue to these constellations of memory. Instances are timeless because they float free of their original context in time; they are patterns because they align with other such moments because each one is the distillation of meaning out of what passes away. In Book IV of the *Confessions*, Augustine writes of beautiful things that come into being and pass away,

> This is the law of their nature. You have endowed them so richly because they belong to a society of things that do not all exist at once, but in their passing away and succession together form a whole, of which the several creatures are parts. So is it with our speaking as it proceeds by audible signs: it will not be a whole utterance unless one word dies away after making its syllables heard, and gives place to another.[13]

Perishable things in time come into their meaning only after they have passed away and become part of a larger form. Any time one understands a sentence, one draws its meaning from the way that its passing words cohere or coalesce in the memory. Eliot writes in the fifth section of "Burnt Norton":

Words move, music moves
Only in time; but that which is only living

13 The *Confessions*, trans. Maria Boulding, O.S.B. New York: New City Press, 2010, p. 66. All subsequent citations will reference the page numbers of this text.

Can only die. Words, after speech, reach
Into the silence. Only by the form, the pattern,
Can words or music reach
The stillness, as a Chinese jar still
Moves perpetually in its stillness. (19)

Creatures in time are "only living," and there is something beyond
living in this sense. "Words, after speech, reach/Into the silence."
Eliot surely does not mean only that the words, once spoken, cease
to be heard, but rather that they reach something that can occur
only after the words have been completed. Eliot goes on to say that
it is not the words themselves or the notes of the music that constitute what reaches into the silence: "Only by the form, the pattern,/Can words or music reach/The stillness, as a Chinese jar
still/Moves perpetually in its stillness" The poem echoes Keats's
lines in "Ode on a Grecian Urn": "Heard melodies are sweet, but
those unheard/Are sweeter" and "Thou, silent form! dost tease us
out of thought/As doth eternity." But Eliot's point is a more pro-
found one. When words or music "reach the stillness," they come
into the presence of "the still point of the turning world" (15), the
"Word in the desert" (19), the Logos, who is like Eliot in not appearing by his human name or by any bodily image in the *Four
Quartets*.[14] Form or pattern emerges as a discovered truth, not as
"knowledge derived from experience" (26)—which is an imposed
and falsified pattern—only because the Logos has entered history
and made possible this discovery.

The account of Augustine's life in the *Confessions*, of course,
illustrates this discovery of the Logos in the form of his experience,
but what Eliot means might perhaps be understood by exploring
one instance of this pattern. In his discussion of time in XI.38, Augustine uses as an example the recitation of a poem he knows by
heart. "Before I begin," he says, "my expectation is directed to the
whole poem, but once I have begun, whatever I have plucked away

14 Despite numerous references to them, the names of Jesus and Mary
    never appear in the four poems. Christ is identified in "The Dry Sal-
    vages" simply as "Incarnation"(44).

from the domain of expectation and tossed behind me to the past becomes the business of my memory, and the vital energy of what I am doing is in tension between the two of them" (245). Actually, though, the experience is still more complicated. Augustine could not recite the poem at all—in other words, his expectation could not be "directed to the whole poem"—unless he already *remembered* it. What he expects in the future is already present in his memory. One might speculate about why he uses the recitation of a memorized poem as his example. Several reasons suggest themselves. First, recitation displays the particular distention of the soul that underlies our experience of time. Second, it gives us an intimation of what it might be like to be at once God and man—that is, fully embedded in time but also knowing what is to come as though it were already the past. And third, the poem locates the meditation on time in a pattern both peculiar to Augustine's life and discernible to his readers. He does not specify which poem he has in mind, but he has just cited the hymn beginning *Deus, creator omnium*, "God, Creator of all" in analyzing long and short syllables in XI.35. Moreover, he has mentioned this hymn before in the *Confessions*. Shortly after his mother's death in IX.32, he describes being displeased with himself at the depth of his grief. He went to sleep, "and on awakening," he says, he "felt a good deal better. As I lay in bed alone I remembered some lines by your servant Ambrose, which rang true for me," and he goes on to quote the first eight lines of *Deus, creator omnium* (178).

When he chooses a particular hymn to use as his example in Book XI, then, this would be naturally be the one to come to mind. He does not mention in Book XI that the poem was written by St. Ambrose, but the fact is important, because it fits into a pattern that begins in Book VI before Monica's death. Whenever he saw Augustine, Ambrose "would often burst out in praise of her," telling Augustine how lucky he was to have such a mother (96). Augustine himself had a somewhat ambivalent relation to Ambrose. Although he first glimpsed the spiritual meaning of difficult passages of Scripture through Ambrose's explications, he was disappointed never to be able to converse with Ambrose in private as he wished: "my inner turmoil was at such a feverish pitch that I needed to find him completely at leisure if I were to pour it all out, and I never did so find him" (97). After his conversion, he experienced still another miss. He wrote to Ambrose "asking his advice as to which [books of the Bible] in particular I ought to read," and Ambrose recommended Isaiah. "The first part I read of this book was incomprehensible to me, however," writes Augustine, "and, assuming that all the rest would be the same, I put it off, meaning to take it up again later, when I was more proficient in the word of the Lord" (165–66). His true encounter with Ambrose comes through the consolation of the poem on the morning after his mother's funeral in Book IX. Unspoken but implicit in the consolation is his knowledge of how much Ambrose revered his mother. The crucial moment takes on its meaning in relation to previous moments, both in what did happen and what did not.

His later imagined recitation in Book XI draws his own history into it as the experience of a pattern. To recite the words *Deus, creator omnium* is to call to mind at least three things: Monica, who gave birth to Augustine, who prayed for him incessantly, who rejoiced at his conversion, and at whose death he found consolation in the recitation of this poem; Ambrose, the author of the poem and the first man to "draw aside the veil of mystery" and open to Augustine the "spiritual meaning" of Scripture (99); and of course the meaning of the words, "God, creator of all." To recite the poem now in a meditation on time is to recall the general relation of God, creator of all, to all that is coming into being and passing away. But it is also to recall His particular creation of Augustine and his own re-creation as a Christian. Augustine reflects that what can be said about the recitation of a poem, which is prolonged until expectation is used up and the whole of it has passed into memory, can also be said of the entirety of a person's life. It can also be said of "the entire sweep of human history, the parts of which are individual human lives" (245). The completion of the pattern is the stillness of form apprehended outside the motion of time, an experience of the Word Himself. Augustine describes the encounter in his account of his conversation with Monica as they stood at a window overlooking a garden in Ostia. At the height of their exaltation they touch the edge of eternal Wisdom, and then "sighing and unsatisfied" they returned "to the noise of articulate speech, where a word has a beginning and an end. How different from your Word, our Lord, who abides in himself, and grows not old, but renews all things" (173–74).

4

Eliot thinks through similar matters in the *Four Quartets*, but without representing particular persons.[15] In Section II of "Burnt Norton," he locates what Augustine calls "that eternal Wisdom who abides above all things" (174),

At the still point of the turning world. Neither flesh nor fleshless;
Neither from nor towards; at the still point, there the dance is,
But neither arrest nor movement. And do not call it fixity,
Where past and future are gathered. Neither movement from nor towards,
Neither ascent nor decline. Except for the point, the still point,
There would be no dance, and there is only the dance.
I can only say, *there* we have been: but I cannot say where.
And I cannot say, how long, for that is to place it in time.

At the still point, which is like the axle of all existence, one is outside the motion of time. Just as there would be no circle without the spaceless point at its center, there would be no motion without the still point: "There would be no dance, and there is only the dance." Already by the end of Section II of "Burnt Norton," Eliot seems to have addressed the problem of unredeemable time brought up at the beginning of the poem:

Time past and time future
Allow but a little consciousness.
To be conscious is not to be in time

15 Except as imaginary encounters with ghostly forms (Section I of "Burnt Norton," Section I of "East Coker," and Section II of "Little Gidding"), Eliot does not represent human beings mimetically, and even on these occasions, there is very little physical description.

But only in time can the moment in the rose-garden,
The moment in the arbour where the rain beat,
The moment in the draughty church at smokefall
Be remembered; involved with past and future.
Only through time time is conquered.

To be conscious in this sense, I think, is to experience something like the moment at the window in Ostia with his mother or the *Tolle lege*, "Take up and read," that Augustine heard in the garden (another garden) under a fig tree, with its recollection of the pear tree of his youth, the original transgression of Eve in being urged to "become as gods," and Christ's recognition of Nathaniel under a fig tree. Yet such timeless moments become redemptive only when they are remembered—that is, gathered out of their temporal sequence—because history is not serial. Rather, "history is a pattern of timeless moments."

The poems of *Four Quartets* come closer to the mode of spiritual confession in Augustine's vein than anything else Eliot wrote. Like Augustine taking stock of his present life in Book X, Eliot has to keep revisiting his own solutions. The principal insight of both Augustine and Eliot lies in their emphasis on glimpsing the pattern, for example, but finding it is no easy matter of concentration and will. As Eliot writes in "East Coker," the second poem of the *Four Quartets*, there is

At best, only a limited value
In the knowledge derived from experience.
The knowledge imposes a pattern, and falsifies,
For the pattern is new in every moment
And every moment is a new and shocking
Valuation of all we have been.

If knowledge itself imposes a false pattern, then what is the alternative? This kind of knowledge, which would seem to resemble what Aristotle calls practical judgment (*phron sis*) or perhaps what Pascal means by *esprit de finesse*. Eliot might mean in general that knowledge from experience "imposes a pattern" if it becomes *conceptual,* as though one could draw distinct rules and principles from it for guiding oneself in the future—the kinds of things that go into motivational books for "success," for example.[16] But his concern seems to be less with action than with thought or self-understanding. If "every moment is a new and shocking/Valuation of all we have been," then one cannot say what one is until the sentence is complete, as it were, and one is no longer in time at all. How, then, can does one discern the "pattern of timeless moments" without imposing a pattern? The problem with knowledge is that it tends toward fixity, unlike the still point "where past and future are gathered." What Eliot calls for, drawing upon such mystics as St. John of the Cross, is a waiting that deliberately renounces the things that seem like answers—hope, love, and thought—because hope and love would have the wrong objects, and "you are not ready for thought" (28). The way has to be "the way of ignorance," "the way of dispossession," "the way in which you are not" (29). It is a way of unknowing in the mystical sense, and certainly the spiritual achievement of what Keats calls "negative capability," when one "is capable of being in uncertainties, Mysteries, doubts without any irritable reaching after fact & reason."[17]

As the implicit protagonist of these poems, Eliot must renounce willful attempts to master his life and make a success of himself. He must wait. But the purpose of the waiting emerges as clearly in the *Four Quartets* as it does in the *Confessions*. As Eliot puts it,

16 In the glossary to his translation of Aristotle's *Ethics*, Joe Sachs writes that he chooses "practical judgment" to translate *phron sis* as "the best way of conveying Aristotle's central understanding that ethical choices can never be deductions from any rules, principles, or general duties, but always require a weighing of particular circumstances and balancing of conflicting principles in a direct recognition of the mean." Aristotle, *Nicomachean Ethics*. Trans. Joe Sachs. Newburyport, MA: Focus Publishing, 2002, p.210.
17 John Keats, Letter to George and Thomas Keats, Dec. 22, 1817. *Letters of John Keats to his Family and Friends*. Ed. Sidney Colvin. Cambridge: Cambridge Library Collection, 2011, p. 48.

The hint half guessed, the gift half understood, is Incarnation.
Here the impossible union
Of spheres of existence is actual,
Here the past and future
Are conquered, and reconciled,
Where action were otherwise movement
Of that which is only moved
And has in it no source of movement—
Driven by daemonic, chthonic
Powers. (44–45)

For Eliot at least, there can be no complete intellectual grasp of the hint and gift that is the Incarnation. Yet only here is time redeemed: "Only through time time is conquered" (16). As Joseph Schwartz writes, "The gift given to mankind is Incarnation. Upon the knowledge of the Incarnation the religious and moral exploration of time and place depends. The whole of the *Quartets* exfoliates from this fact."[18] Knowledge of the Incarnation gives history a focal point; it provides many "timeless moments" in the biography of Jesus, such as the miracles and the events of the Passion; but more importantly, the whole of the human life of Christ, which "ends" only with the Ascension, is in its entirety the "point of intersection of the timeless with time" (44), and as such, it sacralizes human life in all its particularity of time and place. It accepts finite time and a local setting as absolute limitations. Through time, it conquers time.

5

Taken as an event, the Incarnation continues to change everything that comes before it and after it, but its force does not diminish, as though it had only taken place during the period of Christ's earthly life. Its culmination is always the present moment. As Eliot puts it, "So, while the light falls/On a winter's afternoon, in a secluded chapel/History is now and England" (58). Incarnation will not be complete until time itself is complete. But if finitude and "sensuous

18 Schwartz, "Theology of History," 43.

embodiment," in Eliot's phrase, are the conditions both of poetry and of Incarnation, one question stands out about Eliot's mode of his "confessions" in contrast to Augustine's: why he chose abstract, difficult, philosophical poetry as his mode rather than a more concrete poetry or a more personal work on the order of C.S. Lewis' *A Grief Observed*. What does he accomplish in the compromise he makes with pure impersonality in the subdued autobiography of the poem?

One answer lies in what Martin Warner has called the "method of enactment" in the *Four Quartets*, the way in which the poem as a whole presents "human needs and aspirations phenomenologically so that we may apprehend the 'general validity' of the analysis, attempting to present Divine love as fulfilling the criteria thereby established, and challenging a response."[19] Working through the poem, in other words, brings the reader into touch, not with the irrelevant particulars of Eliot's life, but with the essential questions roused by those particulars and shared by the reader who struggles through them. Eliot's concern seems to be simple: to reveal his life as a question about embodied being in time whose answer, enacted over the course of the four poems, is the Incarnation. Another reason for his choice of philosophic poetry might be like Augustine's rejection of rhetoric as a career. As Eliot famously writes in "East Coker," he grows tired of "the intolerable wrestle/With words and meanings" that poetry requires: "The poetry does not matter" (26).

But other reasons for Eliot's mode also suggest themselves. As Hugh Kenner has pointed out, Eliot came upon the form of *The Waste Land* when it was "reconceived from the wreckage of a different conception" and made into something new:

> What survived was a form with no form, and a genre with no name. Years later, on the principle that a form is anything done twice, Eliot reproduced the structural contours of *The Waste Land* exactly, though more briefly,

19 Warner, "Philosophical Poetry," 241.

in "Burnt Norton," and later still three more times, to make the *Quartets*, the title of which points to a decision that such a form might have analogies with music. That was *post facto*.[20]

Kenner sounds unconvinced that these poems are forms at all; "*post facto*" has a note of derision in it. But Eliot's repetition of the five-part structure of *The Waste Land* in the *Four Quartets* might have another justification. Perhaps he means for the five separate poems to constitute a single, increasingly confessional, increasingly ascetic opus of five parts. In that case, "to arrive where we started/And know the place for the first time" (59) would also be to say, "To Carthage then I came" in a new sense. By the time he came to write the *Four Quartets*, which long ago entered and altered the whole tradition of Western literature (subtly changing our reception of Augustine), he had moved away from putting so much stress on poetry per se; instead of the literary tradition as a simultaneous order of great works of art, he was speaking of history as a pattern of timeless moments. He was wary of any hint of mere aestheticism, not that he had ever been given to an isolation of poetry from its moral and religious import. By the beginning of World War II, he was unquestionably most interested in "the fight to recover what has been lost/And found and lost again and again: and now, under conditions/That seem unpropitious." London was burning now as Carthage once had burned; in "Little Gidding," the Nazi buzz bombs are falling. What Augustine had done had to be done again, because the days were evil; the spirit of revenge was loose upon Europe. Then as in Augustine's day, then as in the pressing now of Incarnation, time had to be redeemed.

20 Hugh Kenner, "The Urban Apocalypse" in *Eliot in His Time: Essays on the Occasion of the Fiftieth Anniversary of* The Waste Land." Princeton, Princeton UP, 1973.